UTAH
CANYON
COUNTRY

When the hand of the Creator swept across this land we now call Utah, it did so with elegance and grace, and endowed us with a gift of exquisite beauty.

The Utah Geographic Series is a celebration of this vast landscape which stretches for 85,000 square miles across the state of Utah. The Series will portray in words and photographs the unique diversity of Utah's astounding landforms, colorful history, expansive natural areas and vigorous people.

It is our hope that through the Series, Utahns and visitors alike will develop a deeper understanding and appreciation of the wonder that is Utah.

Rick Reese,
Publisher

Junction Butte,
Canyonlands National Park.
Larry Ulrich

UTAH CANYON COUNTRY

by F. A. BARNES

UTAH GEOGRAPHIC SERIES, INC.

SALT LAKE CITY, UTAH

1986

Second printing, revised, 1987
Design by Jacoby-Reese Design Associates,
Salt Lake City, Utah
Printed in Japan by DNP America, Inc.,
San Francisco, California
Library of Congress Catalog Number 85-52187
ISBN 0-936331-01-1
Published by Utah Geographic Series, Inc.,
Box 8325, Salt Lake City, Utah 84108

CONTENTS

*Cow Canyon, Glen Canyon
National Recreation Area.*

John Telford

FOREWORD

Characterizing what it is that makes Utah so extraordinary can be done in two words: uniquely diverse. Nowhere else on the face of the planet can the juxtaposition of canyons, high plateaus, mountains and desert be found on the scale that it is here. From magnificent alpine peaks to serene farmlands, from the bustle of vital cities to the stark solitude of the Great Basin, from the astoundingly convoluted canyon country to an enormous dead sea, Utah is indeed diverse, unique and stunningly beautiful.

The people who inhabit this land have felt, in the formation of their collective character, the forces of terrain, water and space. And though population distribution makes Utah surprisingly urban, the values of her people are, in the best sense of the word, decidedly rural. Family life, hard work, spiritual values and a commitment to one another is the credo of our people. Utahns are tough, able and no-nonsense. They expect each to take care of his own but can respond with magnanimity in cooperative efforts to dike a flooding city, rebuild a burned-out farmstead and respond to the needs of their neighbors.

The people of Utah love the open space they find here; it is a necessary and integral component of their lives. They expect it and, at times, even take it for granted. The vast-ness of the state has deeply affected the views of her people, and in different, sometimes conflicting ways. To some, the expanse of natural area in Utah is so large that it is regarded as limitless. To those holding this view, open space should be conquered, utilized and developed for economic gain. To others, open space is valued for its beauty and for the high quality of life it affords. For those ascribing to this view, preserving the natural face of our state is paramount. But however it is perceived, open space has vital meaning to the people of Utah.

The Utah Geographic Series is a celebration of all that is Utah: its vast space, its matchless beauty, its absolutely unique diversity and its people. Through images and words, these books will lead us to a deeper understanding and a greater appreciation of our state. *Utah Canyon Country,* the first volume in the series, is a good place to begin.

The canyon country of southeastern Utah was the last region of the American west to yield the secrets of its remarkably rugged geography. Portions of it yet remain unexplored and only partially understood. The intricacy of its landscape leaves it today nearly as secretive and inspiring as during the time of the Anasazi, the "ancient ones" who for centuries dwelt here. In the depths of these gorges, in the flow of intermittent waters, in the incomparable wonder of pervasive silence, lie discoveries each of us seek about ourselves and the land about us.

The Anasazi grew and flourished here. They built cities, farmed the canyons and mesas, pursued a spiritual existence and formed a social order. Then, in an astonishingly short time, they were mysteriously gone. The answer to the demise of the Anasazi may one day come as a shock to modern man as he discerns the true meaning of his relationship to the land and its limits. Let us hope that for us the discovery will not be too late.

The appearance of the Utah Geographic Series fills a long-felt need in Utah, and based upon a quarter-century of close association with its publisher, I know that we can look forward to an illuminating and beautiful portrayal of our magnificent state. Utahns and visitors alike will welcome the knowledge and understanding this series brings. The accompanying sensitivity to and appreciation of our special province of the west will make it a better place for all of us.

Ted Wilson
Salt Lake City
March, 1986

A wildflower graces a sand-stone wall in Canyonlands National Park.
Pat O'Hara

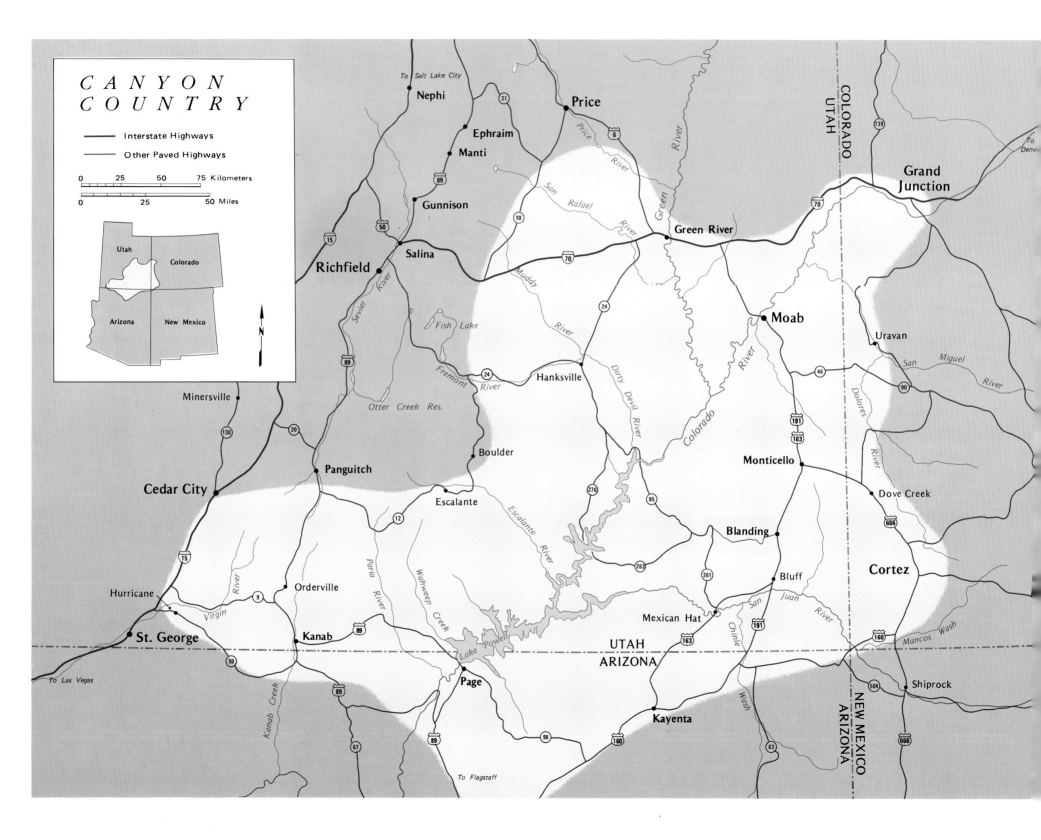

CANYON
COUNTRY

Interstate Highways
Other Paved Highways

0   25   50   75 Kilometers
0   25   50 Miles

Utah   Colorado

Arizona   New Mexico

N

To Salt Lake City

Nephi
Price
31
Ephraim
6
Manti
89
Gunnison
10
Salina
Green River
Green River
Grand Junction
139
To Denver
70
15
50
Richfield
70
Sevier River
Muddy
24
Moab
Uravan
San Rafael River
San Miguel River
90
46
Minersville
Fish Lake
89
Fremont River
24
Hanksville
Dirty Devil River
Colorado River
Dolores River
Otter Creek Res.
130
20
Panguitch
Boulder
276
95
Monticello
Dove Creek
Cedar City
Escalante
12
191
163
666
Escalante River
Blanding
263
281
Cortez
Hurricane
Virgin River
9
Orderville
Paria River
Wahweep Creek
Bluff
261
15
Kanab
89
Mexican Hat
191
160
St. George
59
Lake Powell
San Juan River
Chinle Wash
Mancos Wash
504
Shiprock
Page
UTAH
ARIZONA
666
To Las Vegas
Kanab Creek
89
98
163
Kayenta
160
NEW MEXICO
ARIZONA
67
89
63
To Flagstaff

COLORADO
UTAH

Canyon Country is an immense, sprawling maze of deep canyons and gorges that the Colorado River and its tributaries have cut into the ancient high desert that lies between the Rocky Mountains of western Colorado and the high plateaus of central Utah. It is a part of the Colorado Plateau, a geologic province that occupies the heartland of the Four Corners states of Arizona, Colorado, New Mexico, and Utah.

Canyon Country's geologic boundaries are not always apparent to the casual observer, but it is approximately outlined by the Dolores and Mancos rivers in western Colorado, the base of the high plateaus in central Utah, and the federal and state highways shown on the map.

Most of the terrain that inspired those who named Canyon Country borders the Colorado River and its major tributaries.

Four island mountain ranges loom high above this vast canyon system, and arid expanses of high desert terrain lie between many tributary canyons.

In earlier years, both "Canyon Country" and "Canyonlands" were used to describe this part of the Colorado Plateau, but since Canyonlands National Park was established in 1964, "Canyonlands" has been commonly applied to the park with "Canyon Country" representing the larger region.

Most of Canyon Country lies within the state of Utah, but it extends south into Arizona and east into Colorado. The region's scenic highlights that are readily accessible to the public, however, lie almost entirely in southern Utah and a small portion of western Colorado. Most of Canyon Country land in Arizona is Indian reservation.

Monument Basin, Canyonlands National Park.
F.A. Barnes

WORLD HERITAGE NOMINATION FOR THE COLORADO PLATEAU

The United Nations' Educational, Scientific and Cultural Organization (UNESCO) established the World Heritage program to call attention to the world's unique natural and cultural areas. More than 100 sites have been designated as World Heritage Sites, twelve of them in the United States, including Grand Canyon and Mesa Verde national parks.

Placement of a site on the World Heritage list is a lengthy process which begins with nomination by the country in which the site is located. A UNESCO committee reviews the nomination and grants or denies approval. Approved World Heritage sites are prime travel goals for international travelers.

In the United States, the National Park Service is responsible for nominating areas for World Heritage status. On May 6, 1982, the National Park Service issued this notice:

The Department of the Interior, through the National Park Service, has compiled the following indicative inventory of cultural and natural properties in the United States that, based on preliminary examination, appear to qualify for World Heritage status and that may be considered for nomination to the World Heritage Committee over the next ten years.

The notice listed and described the sites nominated, including seven federal park areas in Canyon Country: Arches, Bryce, Canyonlands, Capitol Reef and Zion national parks and Colorado and Rainbow Bridge national monuments.

On January 2, 1985, Scott Matheson, then governor of Utah, requested that the entire Colorado Plateau be considered for nomination to the World Heritage list under a combined natural and cultural resources theme. In a letter to the National Park Service, Matheson wrote:

I would respectfully like to propose a Thematic World Heritage List Nomination for lands and other resources on the Colorado Plateau region of Utah, Nevada, Arizona, New Mexico and Colorado.

Matheson noted that the erosional landforms of the Colorado Plateau met the nomination criteria by possessing "significant portions of closely related properties," and called attention to the extraordinary cultural resources "associated with the Anasazi, Fremont, and other cultures which existed on the plateau for hundreds of years prior to the European colonization of the Americas."

Matheson then listed 55 special areas totaling more than 6 million acres in the five-state Colorado Plateau region. The Governor was the first to give modern political recognition to something long favored by others—that the entire Colorado Plateau region is worthy of special protection.

View north from Danish Hill, Capitol Reef National Park
F. A. Barnes

I. NATURAL HISTORY

GEOLOGY
PREHISTORIC LIFE
WILDLIFE
PLANT LIFE
SPECIAL ECOSYSTEMS
CLIMATE, WEATHER AND SEASONS

*View of Turret Arch through
North Window Arch,
Arches National Park
Pat O'Hara*

GEOLOGY

The story of Canyon Country is intimately linked to its geology. From its spectacular surface features to its biological communities and human history, the region is connected to the geologic history of the Colorado Plateau. Geologists believe that this immense slab of continental crust was created by some continental drift cataclysm long before the formation of the present continents and probably before the formation of Pangea, the "supercontinent" that split into the land masses presently scattered over the planet. Whatever its origin, this unique geologic region is exceptionally durable, having existed as a distinct entity for at least a half-billion years.

The Colorado Plateau was a part of the land mass now called North America when this continent first began splitting away from Pangea about 150 million years ago. For tens of millions of years following that stupendous breakup, the Plateau was essentially on the west coast of North America, as that continent slowly drifted westward. During that time, the Plateau region was either submerged and accumulating ocean and coastal sediments, or it was above sea level and accumulating freshwater sediments washed down from the higher ground to the east.

With only one minor exception, the oldest geologic strata now exposed within Canyon Country were deposited some 300 million years ago, long before the formation of Pangea. That exception is within the Colorado River gorge near the Colorado-Utah border, where the river has cut into Precambrian rock more than a half-billion years old. This ancient granitic rock was thrust upward by a series of uplifts that began long before the present Rocky Mountains formed.

The geologic strata that have played such an important part in shaping Canyon Country were deposited on the bedrock of the Colorado Plateau over an immense span of time beginning before Pangea formed and persisting for many millions of years after its breakup. Even after the mountain ranges that now lie to the west of the Colorado Plateau were pushed upward by various continental drift activities, seas intruding from other directions left thick marine deposits on top of older Plateau sediments. Freshwater runoff from the mountains that partly surrounded the region continued to build up in the Plateau lowlands until approximately ten million years ago.

Then, the present major phase of erosion began a process that has removed several thousand vertical feet of newer deposits, exposing the older rock and carving the region's deep canyons. Geologists are convinced that this long erosional phase began about ten million years ago because no trace of the Colorado River older than this can be found in its birthplace in the Rocky Mountains.

This erosional phase began when a continental drift event (that may still be continuing) lifted the entire western half of North America a mile upward. This increase in elevation brought more precipitation to the Rockies and produced enough runoff to create permanent rivers and streams in the arid region to the west. In time, that elevated region, surrounded by even higher mountains, was eroded deeply enough to permit its entrenched rivers and streams to reach older and harder strata. The mighty Colorado River and its tributaries then began carving the complex maze of gorges that make the region unique.

Canyons do not readily form in all geologic strata that are now exposed in Canyon Country; some strata are too soft or too thin to permit canyon forming. Most of the canyons have formed in rock strata deposited either before or during the 120 million years when the Colorado Plateau was part of Pangea. This long phase of relative geologic inactivity permitted the deposition of thick, fairly uniform layers of sediments, the kind that in time became rock favorable for canyon forming. The thicker layers were either desert-dune or ocean-shore sands with thinner layers of marine or freshwater sediments separating them. The older geologic strata that are presently exposed in the region are interlayered shallow-marine and shoreline deposits.

The canyons that form in the region's massive sandstones generally have nearly perpendicular walls because such rock shears off in a near-vertical plane when undercut by flowing water. Canyons in older, more layered strata generally have steeply terraced walls.

The island mountain ranges in Canyon Country are of a unique type, best described as volcanoes that did not quite make it. During periods of unusual geologic activity, hot magma was thrust up within the rock strata of the Colorado Plateau in several places, four of them in Canyon Country. In these four places the molten rock did not

THE GREAT DESERT PERIOD

Two hundred million years ago, Canyon Country was a region of low, featureless plains on the west coast of the supercontinent Pangea. For most of the next forty million years the region was a vast Sahara-like desert, with the dominant desert dunes giving way for only relatively short periods of time.

With some exceptions, the deposits laid down in Canyon Country during this time were Wingate Sandstone, the Kayenta Formation, Navajo Sandstone, the Carmel Formation, and Entrada Sandstone. The Wingate, Navajo, and Entrada sandstones were all originally desert-dune sands. The Kayenta and Carmel formations represent periods of

wetter climate, when the sand dunes were buried under freshwater sediments.

There was also a period when the surface of the land eroded away. The depth of the desert dune deposits varied from area to area, but even after the extended period of erosion, Navajo Sandstone remained more than 2,000 feet thick in western Canyon Country.

This great desert period played a vital role in shaping Canyon Country. Most of the region's cliff-forming geologic strata are composed of the "petrified dune" deposits left during those forty million years. The intervening layers of water-deposited sediments

influenced the shaping of the cliffs and helped create many of the region's arches and natural bridges.

Cliffs representative of the great desert period dominate Arches, Zion, and Canyonlands national parks, most of Lake Powell, stretches of the Colorado, Green, and Dolores river gorges in Canyon Country, and the immense monocline "reefs" of Capitol Reef National Park, the San Rafael Swell, and Comb Ridge. The cliffs and spires of Monument Valley formed from much older De Chelly Sandstone, another thick desert-dune deposit.

Above left: Black Arch, Arches National Park
F.A. Barnes

Above right: Castle Arch, Horse Canyon, Canyonlands National Park
F.A. Barnes

Opposite, above: Paul Bunyan's Potty, Canyonlands National Park
Tom Till

reach the surface, but it did bulge the overhead rock strata upward into mighty uplifts. During the succeeding millions of years, erosion slowly removed the fractured rock above these mountain-sized igneous intrusions. The island ranges in Canyon Country are the remnants of these volcanoes that "died aborning."

The La Sal, Abajo, and Henry mountain ranges and Navajo Mountain formed at different times but in the same manner. Had the hot magma reached the surface, it would have formed a volcano, but Canyon Country strata were so thick that the magma ex-

pended its remaining energy making more sills and bulging them upward to form "laccoliths," Greek for "stone cisterns."

When they first formed, the laccolithic ranges probably resembled high, rounded hills rather than the rugged peaks they have become. The change began about ten million years ago, with the beginning of the present major erosion cycle. Glaciers helped shape the higher slopes during periods of cooler, wetter climate.

Since then, almost 5,000 feet of sediments have eroded from Canyon Country, including the highly fractured rock

above the laccolithic intrusions. This left the granite-like igneous cores exposed and decomposing. The soaring, treeless upper slopes of the La Sal Mountains are typical results of this process. Such "intrusive" igneous rock is also exposed in the Henry and Abajo mountains, but at Navajo Mountain the parent stock and its laccoliths are still deeply buried. Little of the overlying sedimentary rock is left in the La Sal Mountains, but more remains in the Henry and Abajo ranges.

The unique nature of Canyon Country laccolithic ranges has contributed to their

novel appearance and beauty. Rain and snow-melt from the higher slopes have cut deep, complex canyons into the angled sandstone strata that surround them, and in some places stupendous, sharply tilted slabs of colorful sandstone lie on their bases. Such slabs are particularly outstanding on the northern slopes of Navajo Mountain and around the southern peaks of the Henry Mountains. These remnants of past geologic events are best viewed from the air, but those on Navajo Mountain are also visible from Lake Powell in the vicinity of Oak Creek Bay. Excellent examples in the Henrys are visible from the state highway leading to Bullfrog Basin.

Because they are higher than the rest of Canyon Country, the region's laccolithic ranges capture more moisture from passing storm systems. This water, whether it flows rapidly on the surface into rivers, streams and reservoirs or slowly through underground strata into subterranean aquifers or to springs, has always been vital to the plant and animal life native to the region and to its human occupants.

Were it not for its strange mountains, Canyon Country would be habitable by only a few hardy desert species, and many of its

HOW ARCHES AND NATURAL BRIDGES FORM

The sandstone formations of Canyon Country vary in composition and in thickness. When exposed on the surface, they respond to various span-forming forces in different ways. Some sandstones absorb water, while others are impermeable and act as barriers to water. These factors and others work together in a complex fashion to produce the different kinds of natural rock spans found in Canyon Country.

Flowing water can undercut a sandstone cliff. If the cliff is a relatively thin wall between canyons or between loops of the same canyon, the water will eventually cut through the wall and be diverted through the short tunnel it has shaped, thus leaving a "natural bridge." Slower kinds of water erosion enlarge the original opening, in time destroying the bridge. There are natural bridges in all stages of formation, aging, and collapse in Canyon Country.

Rain water and snow-melt that are absorbed into porous sandstones play an active part in forming most natural arches. This water seeps slowly downward until it reaches an impervious sandstone layer and then travels laterally. If the water surfaces in a canyon wall, it weakens the sandstone, causing granules, layers, and even large pieces to fall away. In time, this may form an arch in the cliff. This is a common type of arch in Canyon Country.

Other factors also contribute to the formation of natural spans, such as two kinds of exfoliation or cracking along stress planes; but water is the greatest factor in the formation, shaping, and ultimate destruction of Canyon Country natural spans.

At one time many people believed that wind played a vital part in the forming and shaping of this region's arches and natural bridges, but geologists have shown that such is not the case.

most magnificent canyons would not exist.

The several non-mountainous highlands in Canyon Country are the remnants of other types of geologic uplifts. Most of these highlands are somewhat oval in shape, like gigantic blisters, with the more highly fractured rock in their centers removed by eons of erosion that have left stupendous walls of tilted rock strata outlining the uplifts. The centers of the larger uplifts have also been slashed deeply by erosion, adding their own canyon systems to those created by the region's major rivers.

"Uplift" refers to an enormous, oval bulge in relatively level geological strata. During its long geologic history, Canyon Country has been affected by a number of uplifts, but the remnants of only five are presently visible: the Uncompahgre Uplift in western Colorado, the Circle Cliffs Uplift and San Rafael Swell in Utah, and the Echo Cliffs and Monument uplifts in Utah and Arizona. The Uncompahgre, which may still be growing, began forming about 310 million years ago, thrust upward several times and was last active about one million years ago. The cause of these uplifts is not precisely known, but current theory indicates a probable relationship with continental drift activities. For example, some Uncompahgre uplift periods appear to correspond to specific continental drift events.

The Circle Cliffs, Echo Cliffs, Monument, and San Rafael uplifts share certain characteristics. They are visible on the surface as oval "reefs" of tilted, harder sandstone strata many miles long, with their interiors eroded into magnificent canyon systems. In all four, the eastern reefs, or monoclines, are much more obvious and sharply tilted than their western perimeters, a characteristic more apparent from the air than from the highways that cross them.

Interstate 70, between Green River and Salina, slices through the eastern monocline of the San Rafael Swell, climbs onto its central highlands, crosses the broad meadows and deep canyons there, and then descends through its gently sloped western perimeter of colorful sandstones.

In Capitol Reef National Park, the reef is the eastern monocline of the Circle Cliffs Uplift. Utah 24 cuts across this uplift parallel to the Fremont River. Its western perimeter is obscured by the Aquarius Plateau, but parts of it are visible north of Escalante.

Utah 95 crosses the Monument Uplift south of the Abajo Mountains, west of Blanding, and U.S. 191 angles through it between Bluff, Utah, and Kayenta, Arizona, as it goes through Monument Valley. Both highways cut through Comb Ridge, the steeply tilted eastern reef of the immense uplift. The western monocline of the uplift is less conspicuous and is totally obscured in places, but it is visible from both Utah 95 in Utah, and from U.S. 160 in Arizona.

One monocline of the Echo Cliffs Uplift is visible as a line of cliffs to the east of Navajo Bridge, where U.S. 89A crosses the Colorado River.

The visible part of the gigantic Uncompahgre Uplift angles southeastward from Grand Junction, Colorado; Colorado National Monument is located high on this end of the uplift. The uplift's western slopes

CLIFF AND SPIRE FORMING

Most rock formations in Canyon Country are either too soft or too thin to form cliffs, but a few are hundreds of feet thick and have the properties necessary for the formation of the cliffs and spires. These more massive sandstones originated either as desert dunes or as ocean beaches and sandbars. They may vary in thickness from 100 to 2,300 feet and are composed of relatively uniform granules of sand cemented together by minerals carried by seeping water.

Such sandstones are weaker in some ways than other types of sandstone. They are strong under compression, but they cannot bear their own weight under tension or shear. When undercut, they tend to crack along near-vertical planes and collapse, creating the cliffs common within Canyon Country. If a cliff is curving, as in a canyon bend, that will affect how nearly vertical the sandstone will shear away. Other factors also affect this cliff-forming process, such as fractures or irregularities within the rock.

A cliff-forming rock layer may be undercut by seeping or flowing water or by rain water eroding away a softer layer beneath it. If the undercutting is caused by seeping water, this wetting may permit the formation of a seep-cave, with the weight of the overhead rock slowly redistributed to each side of the cave, which may prevent massive collapse.

When a cliff-forming sandstone develops a relatively thin wall, the wall may collapse selectively, leaving one or more slender sandstone spires, perhaps as tall as the sandstone formation is thick. There are many such spectacular spires in Canyon Country, with excellent examples in Monument Valley and the northern part of Canyonlands National Park.

Other types of spires found in the region are shaped by rain from softer water-deposited sediments, as in Bryce Canyon National Park, or from slowly eroding sandstone "fins," as in Arches National Park.

loom above the Dolores River from about Uravan, Colorado to the river's confluence with the Colorado River. Colorado 141 parallels the Dolores River for many miles, offering views of the uplift's lofty, wooded summit. The Uncompahgre has played a vital part in the shaping of Canyon Country. During earlier eras, it contributed sediments to the older, red-hued geologic strata of Canyon Country. More recently, water runoff from the lofty uplift helped carve the region's canyons. Its hard core and continued activity diverted several rivers, including the Colorado, into new courses.

The Colorado River once ran through Unaweep Canyon, to the east of Gateway, Colorado. The river had cut this gorge through the ancient, granitic core of the uplift, but it was diverted to the north by a complex process called "stream piracy." The Colorado has now cut deeply enough in its new course to once again reach the hard core of the Uncompahgre.

Canyon Country—the land of canyons—is the product of more than a half-billion years of geologic activity and ten million years of massive erosion. This process continues, but at a pace barely discernible on the time scale of human affairs.

Pothole on Grand View Point

Opposite: Waterpockets and reeds at Murphy Point, Canyonlands National Park

POTHOLES

Rainwater and melting snow make depressions in the upper surfaces of most Canyon Country sandstones by dissolving binding minerals and thus loosening surface sand granules. Irregularities in the sandstone may serve to start the process, and winter freezing may hasten it. The loosened sand subsequently washes or blows away, deepening the shallow hole, a slow but continual process. Such "potholes" are common in sandstones composed of desert-dune and ocean shoreline deposits. They occur on fairly level expanses of rock, but also on terraces, in drainage lines, and even on top of the rounded sandstone domes and fins that are so plentiful in Canyon Country.

Most potholes are only a few inches deep and a few feet across, but some grow large enough to host their own plant communities. A few become enormous, perhaps fifty feet across and ten feet deep, and others grow deeper than they are wide. Favorably located large potholes may collect and hold water for months or even year around.

Even shallow potholes can contain transient communities of animal species that have adapted to brief life cycles, some only hours long. A cycle begins when rainwater collects in the depression during warm weather. Eggs and larvae that have been lying dormant and dehydrated in the pothole sediments, perhaps for years, waken and rush through their growth and reproductive cycles, leaving their next generations in the drying bottom sediments. Some of these "cryptobiotic" life forms are unique to Canyon Country.

When a deeper pothole that holds a significant amount of water is near a cliff face, the downward-seeping water generally forms a seep-cave in the cliff face below the pothole. Some of these caves host their own hanging gardens. When a pothole breaks through into a seep-cave it has created, the remaining span of rock is called a "pothole arch," a fairly common formation in Canyon Country.

PREHISTORIC LIFE

The fossilized remnants of the prehistoric life that once occupied Canyon Country range from the primitive shallow marine plants and animals of the Pennsylvanian period (320 to 280 million years ago), through the early reptiles and insect life of the Permian period (280 to 225 million years ago), to the more highly developed life forms of the Triassic and Jurassic periods (225 to 136 million years ago.)

During most of the following Cretaceous period, Canyon Country was inundated by a deep, stagnant sea. When that sea retreated, it left layered seashore and freshwater deposits covering thick sea-bottom sediments, but erosion has removed most of these newer deposits.

Paleontologists and paleobotanists have found much to interest them in the fossil remnants of prehistoric life in Canyon Country, partly because the remnants are older than those commonly found elsewhere in North America. Marine fossils can be found in the older strata, deposited when the Colorado Plateau was alternately shallow sea and low coastal plains and swamps. Some fossils represent a significant part of the "age of reptiles," and there are fossils of tideland creatures left from the seashore deposits of the late Cretaceous period. The invading sea was so deep and stagnant that it harbored relatively little marine life, and its remaining deposits contain few fossils.

The surface of Canyon Country is thus dominated by deposits and fossils from the Pennsylvanian, Permian, Triassic, Jurassic, and Cretaceous periods. There are few remnants of newer geologic strata within the region, and older strata are exposed in only a few places.

The traces of prehistoric life most commonly found in Canyon Country are marine fossils, petrified reptile bones, petrified footprints, and petrified plant fossils. The most obvious fossil remains are petrified trees. There are several petrified forests in the region, at least one of which contains fossils of the earliest true trees, a species of primitive conifer.

The most common fossils found in Canyon Country's Pennsylvanian and Cretaceous deposits are the shells of various kinds of marine clams, oysters and snails; the petrified skeletal remains of crinoids, a flower-like sea animal, and the imprints of hordes of smaller sea creatures.

Most of the animal fossils found in land deposits of the Triassic and Jurassic periods are the petrified bones of early to mid-stage dinosaurs and other reptiles and their footprints preserved in petrified freshwater stream sediments. Some such sites include what may be the tracks of early pterosaurs, or flying reptiles.

The petrified wood found in the region ranges in age from the fossilized trunks of ancient palms and cycads to remnants of the earliest true trees to later trees that grew in the vast swamp-forests of the mid-Triassic period. There are fossils of smaller plants, but they are not obvious to the untrained eye. The remains of prehistoric life more recent than the early Cretaceous period, about 100 million years ago, are rare in Canyon

Opposite above left: Fence Canyon dinosaur tracks
Margaret Malm

Opposite above right: The chuckwalla, a large herbivorous lizard found only along the Colorado River
Stewart Aitchison

Opposite lower left: Horned lizard
Norman Shrewsbury

Opposite lower right: 300 million-year-old brachiopod fossils along the San Juan River
Stewart Aitchison

MAJOR DIVISIONS OF GEOLOGIC TIME

LIFE ERAS	MILLION YEARS AGO	GEOLOGIC PERIODS
CENOZOIC ERA (Age of Recent Life, including mammals and flowering plants)		Quaternary Period
	—2—	Tertiary Period
	—65—	
MESOZOIC ERA (Age of Medieval Life, including reptiles and dinosaurs)		Cretaceous Period
	—136—	Jurassic Period
	—195—	Triassic Period
	—225—	
		Permian Period
	—280—	Pennsylvanian Period
	—320—	
PALEOZOIC ERA (Age of Ancient Life, including fishes, amphibians, and insects)		Mississippian Period
	—345—	Devonian Period
	—395—	Silurian Period
	—435—	Ordovician Period
	—500—	Cambrian Period
	—570—	
PRE-CAMBRIAN ERA		

Country because erosion has removed most of these geologic deposits during the last ten million years.

The dinosaurs that once inhabited Canyon Country left behind their footprints and bones in deposits of the freshwater streams and vast swamps of the Mesozoic Era. This "age of dinosaurs" lasted some 160 million years, and smaller reptiles existed much earlier.

During most of the Mesozoic, the Canyon Country region was barely above sea level and was much nearer the equator than it is now, giving it a hot, humid climate favorable to profuse plant life. This ideal environment for reptiles was interrupted to some extent during the hot and arid great desert period, but even then some reptile species were found here.

The entire Mesozoic Era is represented by geologic strata in Canyon Country, from the oldest, the Moenkopi Formation of the lower Triassic Period, through all the other formations of the Triassic and Jurassic periods, and finally to the youngest, the members of the Mesa Verde Group and other formations of the upper Cretaceous Period. There is not much evidence of land life from the Cretaceous Period in Canyon Country because most of the region was inundated by an invading sea for about 60 million years.

Land life of the Mesozoic Era left traces in the form of petrified bones and footprints. The footprints of reptiles are fairly common in the Moenkopi Formation but other remnants of early life are rare. Bones of the first true dinosaurs occur in the Chinle Formation of the upper Triassic and are fairly common within the Morrison, Cedar Mountain, and Burro Canyon formations of the upper Jurassic and lower Cretaceous. Bones are also found in upper Cretaceous sediments deposited after the sea retreated.

The Morrison Formation provides a rich record of the dinosaurs that occupied Canyon Country. Several major paleontological excavations have been made in the formation's vast freshwater swamp deposits, including those in the Cleveland Lloyd Dinosaur Quarry in the San Rafael Swell. The developed quarry in Dinosaur National Monument on the northern border of the Colorado Plateau is also in the Morrison Formation. Other exceptional sites have been discovered in this formation but have not yet been excavated.

The petrified footprints of prehistoric reptiles have been found many places in Canyon Country, with known sites ranging in age from those in the Moenkopi, about 220 million years old, to some in the Dakota Formation, about 130 million years old. Between these extremes, the petrified footprints of dinosaurs and other reptiles have been found in the Kayenta Formation, in the Moab member of Entrada Sandstone and in the Morrison Formation.

The petrified footprints of smaller animals, including some believed to be those of early pterosaurs, or flying reptiles, have been discovered in desert playa sediments within Navajo Sandstone which was deposited as dune sand when the region was a vast, arid desert. Scientists have yet to explain the presence of these strange creatures in a desert environment. Samples of these footprints, which were discovered nearby, are on exhibit at the museum in Moab, Utah. Another exposure was later found about thirty miles from Moab.

Paleontologists are fascinated by the petrified bones of reptiles, because they can be used to reconstruct, identify, and study prehistoric species. Petrified footprints are not as useful for this purpose, but trackways, or several footprints in sequence, can be studied for clues about reptile weight, walking and running gaits, skeletal structure, and even social behavior when the footprints of several individuals are found in one location.

Wild buckwheat, Monument Valley
Stewart Aitchison

Bird tracks in sand, Coral Pink Sand Dunes State Park
Gerry Ellis

The colorful male collared lizard
Stewart Aitchison

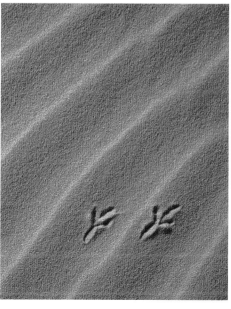

*Prongborn fawns in early
autumn*
John P. George

Long-eared owl
John P. George

The common rock squirrel
Stewart Aitchison

*Mating sphinx moths, Escalante
River Basin*
Larry Ulrich

Caterpillar
Norman Shrewsbury

*A bighorn ram along the Shafer
Trail, Canyonlands National
Park*
Stewart Aitchison

WILDLIFE

Wildlife in Canyon Country can be divided into general communities according to the varying amounts of water and vegetation within the region.

At the lower elevations, perennial rivers such as the Colorado, Green, Dolores, and San Juan host a variety of fish, including catfish, carp, and other muddy-water species, some of which range into the region's larger tributary streams. Smaller rivers with highly variable flow contain smaller fish species that can tolerate the drastic seasonal changes. Most intermittent streams at lower elevations contain no fish but do host a variety of other lifeforms. The small lakes and streams in the region's higher terrain generally contain trout, but because of sport-fishing the trout population in most of these areas must be maintained by periodic restocking.

Lake Powell, in the Glen Canyon National Recreation Area, harbors a wide variety of fish species, most of them native river and stream dwellers that have adapted to the reservoir environment. These include species of catfish, carp, bass, trout, shad, perch, bluegill, sunfish, and crappie. Fish species not native to Canyon Country, such as northern pike, have also mysteriously appeared in the reservoir in recent years.

Other wildlife is found at Lake Powell and the region's lower rivers and streams. Aquatic birds such as ducks, geese, herons, egrets, grebes, blackbirds, bitterns, curlews, and kingfishers abound, some of them as regular inhabitants, others as seasonal visitors. Beaver have built dams in flowing streams, while others have adapted to free-swimming lives in the region's lakes, reservoirs, and rivers.

The river and stream banks, and the marshlands occasionally associated with them, are home to amphibians, water-loving snakes, and a wide variety of rodent species. Mule deer, desert sheep, and other animals also visit these sources of water, but they generally live on higher ground.

The semi-arid desert country above the main water courses harbors a variety of wildlife, including coyotes, foxes, skunks, bobcats, badgers, mule deer, pronghorn antelope, desert sheep, bats, rabbits, porcupines, prairie dogs, ferrets, weasels, and martens, although some of these are quite rare. There are also numerous species of smaller rodents, such as squirrels, chipmunks, gophers, rats, and mice; reptiles, such as lizards and snakes; amphibians, such as toads and frogs; and birds, such as eagles, hawks, owls, falcons, ravens, and magpies.

The insect world is also well represented in this high-desert region, with scorpions, dragonflies, moths, spiders, butterflies, wasps, bees, ants, beetles, flies, and tiny gnats. There are also a few species that are found nowhere else, such as a mosquito whose life cycle is tied to slickrock potholes. Other mosquito species are also common near water in the region.

Elk, puma, bear, marmot, pica, and vole live in the higher elevations of the region's mountains, plateaus, and uplifts, but some are rare or are found only in a few areas.

A herd of free-ranging bison lives in the foothills of one island mountain range, confined to a relatively small area by the surrounding desert. Many of the animal species that inhabit the arid lower country also live in the more heavily vegetated higher elevations.

The wildlife in Canyon Country is as richly varied as that found in less arid life zones of North America, but the casual visitor may see little of it because so many resident species have adapted to nocturnal living to avoid the intense sunlight and desert heat that prevails for much of the year. During the day no life may be evident in the dry canyons that are so common to the region, yet tracks in the sandy dry washes tell of canyon dwellers who venture out in the cool of night.

PLANT LIFE

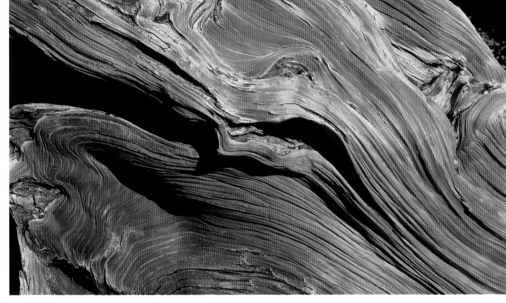

Utah Juniper berries,
Escalante River Basin
Fred Hirschmann

Bristlecone pine at Yovimpa
Point, Bryce Canyon National
Park
Tom Till

The plant life in Canyon Country is divided into general communities according to elevation and several special communities that are unique to the region. The general life zones based on elevation are not sharply defined but overlap to some extent, with the plant species in each zone gradually phasing into the species in adjacent higher and lower zones.

The lowest life zone in the region ranges from 3,500 to 7,500 feet above sea level. The plants that dominate in this zone are pinion-pine, Utah juniper, sagebrush species, greasewood, blackbrush, mountain mahogany, rabbitbrush, Mormon tea, desert holly, cliff-rose, saltbush, snakeweed, pad and barrel cacti, several types of yucca, and a variety of

grasses. The smaller plant species in the zone include a large number of annuals, some of which germinate and complete their brief life cycles only in those years when enough moisture is available.

Within this pinion-juniper life zone, the banks of rivers and streams have their own plant communities, which include cotton-woods, native river willows, and a variety of smaller plants. Boxelder trees and swamp-loving plants, such as cattails, can be found beside springs and canyon streams and in river bottoms. Since cottonwood trees require a steady water supply, their presence in seemingly arid locations indicates that there is ample underground water.

In much of the region, tamarisk, a species

of water-loving, shrubby tree native to north Africa, has become firmly established along river and stream banks and even at many desert springs. There are also isolated communities of ponderosa pine, remnants of a period of wetter climate that is still phasing out.

Another special plant community common to this life zone occurs within the many seep-caves found in sandstone cliffs. Ferns and many other small water-loving plants cling to the crevices from which water slowly seeps, and other plants thrive on any water that may drip or flow down the cliff.

In the life zone that ranges from about 7,000 to 8,500 feet in elevation, the dominant plants are Gambel's oak, aspen, squaw

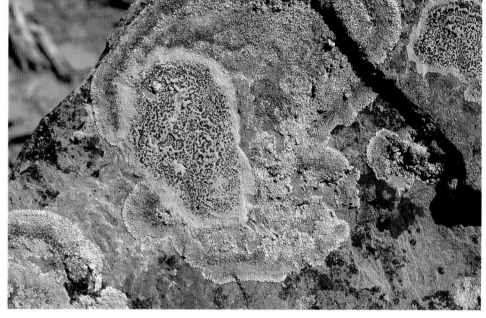

bush, mountain mahogany, a few species of yucca and cacti, gooseberry, raspberry, serviceberry, snowberry, wild rose, and a variety of other brushy species, grasses, and annuals. Red-barked manzanita bush can be found in some locations. The lakes and streams in these elevations also host the same kinds of water-loving plants found in other parts of North America.

Between 8,000 and 10,500 feet the principal plants are aspen, willow, conifers such as spruce, pine and fir, sedges, and a variety of shrubs, grasses, and annuals.

Conifers dominate the 10,000- to 12,000-foot zone, with some carryover of plant species from lower zones. The alpine tundra life zone above 12,000 feet is not

common in Canyon Country but it does exist in the La Sal Mountains. In this zone, the only plants are hardy, low-growing shrubs, such as sedges, grasses, mosses, and the same kinds of alpine plants that grow at this elevation elsewhere on the continent.

Hardy mosses thrive in all Canyon Country life zones. Most grow near sources of moisture, but some varieties manage to survive in sheltered places in otherwise arid areas where they receive moisture only when rain or snow falls.

The lichen species that add a colorful patina to most rock surfaces in the region vary with elevation. In vast areas of the region where sandstone is exposed, such "slickrock" surfaces may be almost entirely

covered with pale-hued lichen with virtually no bare rock visible at higher elevations where exposed rock often blazes with the vivid colors of brighter-hued lichen species.

Species of fungus also thrive throughout the region's life zones. There are even varieties that have adapted to the most arid desert areas, living underground most of the time and showing special growths on the surface only during brief periods when conditions are favorable for sporing.

Cactus flowers, Colorado River gorge
F.A. Barnes

Lichen
F.A. Barnes

In addition to its generalized biological communities and transient cryptobiotic pothole life, Canyon Country has several special ecosystems, including the plant and animal communities associated with seep-caves, intermittent streams, and cryptogamic soils.

Seep-caves form when water from lateral seepage in permeable rock reaches a cliff face, a common occurrence in Canyon Country. This seepage may be channeled laterally by an impervious rock layer from some distance away, may come from an overhead pothole, or may be from a combination of these sources. When the seeping moisture reaches a surface, it weakens the sandstone, causing it to slough away in granules, flakes, and chunks, slowly creating a shallow cave.

This moistened sandstone alcove becomes an ideal environment in which a few kinds of small water-loving plants can take root and grow on an otherwise arid canyon wall. Certain species of mosses, grasses, and ferns plus columbines, orchids, and other annuals thrive in these "hanging gardens," together with small animals, insects, and a few transient birds.

There are thousands of seep caves in Canyon Country. Most canyons have one or more, and a few have so many seeps that their combined flows create streams.

Perennial or intermittent streams in sandstone canyons harbor special ecosystems, each a little different from the other. Perennial flow can support water-loving plant and animal life that cannot survive when a stream diminishes to intermittent flow or flows mostly below the surface. There are, however, species of fish and other tiny aquatic creatures that continue to thrive when a flowing stream is reduced to isolated pools, and there are species of trees and other large plants that can survive on small amounts of subsurface water after the course of a seasonal stream seemingly has become a dry, rocky gully.

Cryptogamic soils or crusts form the basis of the pinion-juniper life zone that dominates the more arid expanses of Canyon Country. The loose, sandy soils in this zone are bound against water and wind erosion by tight crusts composed of complex subsurface communities of fungi, algae, lichens, mosses and diatoms. Little is known about these communities. Cryptogamic crust may be several inches thick and vary in color from gray-green to black. Its surface is generally irregular, often resembling miniature rolling hills or sharp-peaked mountains.

While cryptogamic crusts bind sandy soils against natural erosion and provide a basis for the rest of the life community, they are fragile and easily broken by wheels, human feet and the hooves of ranging domestic livestock. Once this protective crust is broken, erosion can attack the entire local ecosystem, ultimately destroying or drastically changing it by carrying away the scant soil. Damaged cryptogamic crust recovers very slowly, and only if it is undisturbed and not washed or blown away.

In much of Canyon Country, cryptogamic crusts are the basis of all other life. Without them, there would be far fewer plant and animal species in the pinion-juniper life zone. Rolling, living sand dunes, now quite scarce in the region, would dominate as they already do in much of the San Rafael Desert. And with a sparse plant community, water erosion would be far more destructive to both nature and to the works of man. Canyon Country cannot afford to have its cryptogamic soils damaged or destroyed, yet little is being done to study or preserve them.

Seeping springs on wall of
Navajo Sandstone, Escalante
River Basin
Fred Hirschmann

Opposite: Emerald Pools, Zion
National Park
John Telford

CLIMATE

As might be expected in high desert, the climate in Canyon Country is generally semi-arid, although the higher terrain receives more precipitation, depending on its elevation. Most of the region lies between 3,500 and 6,500 feet above sea level and is relatively arid. Within this elevation range, however, extreme irregularities in the land and the high country that immediately surrounds the region combine to create considerable variation in rainfall and snowfall.

The dynamics of natural precipitation from moisture-laden clouds are strongly affected by variations in the surface of the land, especially the mountain ranges, high plateaus, and ridges that lie across the normal paths of storm systems. Exceptionally low areas, such as large valleys and canyons, add further complications. Over the centuries, these geographic features have created localized climate zones within Canyon Country that deviate considerably from the semi-arid norm. In most of the region, the climate varies from extremely dry, with an average of less than three inches total annual precipitation, to as much as ten inches or more in a few areas.

Within the relatively few areas of Canyon Country that lie above 6,500 feet, the climate is less variable and more closely related to similar elevation zones at the same latitude elsewhere in North America. In these areas, there are higher average levels of precipitation and, hence, wetter climates. Above 6,500 feet the changing plant and animal communities provide evidence of this increased precipitation as aspen and other water-loving trees phase rapidly into verdant evergreen forests.

In those areas of the region that lie above 12,000 feet, there is plentiful rain during the warmer months and heavy snow during the rest of the year. In some years the snow pack in a few locations, such as on certain protected slopes in the La Sal Mountains, may last all year. If such snows persist, in time they can become glaciers, as the slowly but continually changing climate produces favorable conditions. This has happened in Canyon Country several times within the last million years and it will undoubtedly happen again.

While Canyon Country is generally considered to be semi-arid, its climate actually ranges from extremely dry, to quite wet, to near-arctic.

Winter sunset in lower Castle Valley, Utab
F.A. Barnes

WEATHER

The weather in Canyon Country varies from day to day and from area to area. Temperatures can range from below zero to 115° Fahrenheit, but these extremes are uncommon. In most of the region temperatures range from 15 °F to 100 °F. Elevation and the broken character of the land affect the day-to-day weather and temperature just as they do the long-range average levels of precipitation.

While the general climate of most of the region is semi-arid, weather is often difficult to predict in Canyon Country. The land is simply too irregular, too extreme in profile, and it creates its own local weather anomalies. But this irregularity also has advantages. For example, it does not permit the formation of tornadoes. The few tornadoes reported have been small, and all have formed within the few broad, open areas in the western part of the region.

The weather in Canyon Country ranges from bright, sunny, and windless to overcast and either calm, windy, or spectacularly stor-

Autumn at Capitol Reef
National Park
F.A. Barnes

ny. On the average, during perhaps 90 percent of the year, the region's weather is sunny, with the few exceptions due to anomalies created by irregular terrain.

This bright serenity is disturbed only by passing storms, the majority of which originate over the Pacific Ocean. Most such storm systems pass to the north or south of Canyon Country or touch it lightly. Only a few storms hit the region directly, but those that do usually cause strong local winds and drop large amounts of water very quickly along a relatively narrow path, often causing violent flooding.

About once a year, a storm system from the Gulf of Mexico reaches parts of Canyon Country. These rare storms usually lie over the region for several days, drenching the land with a slow but steady drizzle. They bring only light to moderate winds and little destructive flooding, but they can raise the flow of the region's major rivers to abnormal levels.

Winter view from Dead Horse
Point State Park
David Muench

Near Cannonville, Utah
Rick Graetz

*Thunderhead over the
Black Box country of the San
Rafael Swell*
Stewart Aitchison

FLASH FLOODS

Surface soils in Canyon Country range from loose, shifting sand or sediments to rich forest loam, with broad expanses of solid rock in many regions. Rain in areas with heavy plant growth is generally absorbed with little or no immediate runoff, but where vegetative cover is sparse, rapid surface runoff can create flash flooding.

Several major factors affect the potential for such destructive flooding, including the amount and rate of rainfall, the ability of the surface soil to absorb the falling water, the amount and type of vegetation growing on that surface, the depth of the absorbent surface soil above a rock layer, and the general slope of the terrain.

In most of Canyon Country, these factors are favorable to flash flooding. During the colder months, snow lies frozen on the ground or slowly melts and is absorbed, but most rainfall in the region is from thunderstorms that drop large amounts of rain along a relatively narrow path. Such heavy precipitation cannot be absorbed fast enough and it runs off rapidly, causing the violent flooding common to all deserts.

Occasionally during late winter, warm winds enter Canyon Country from lower desert areas to the south or west. In a very short time, these winds can melt all the snow and ice below 7,000 feet, and can accelerate melting at higher elevations. In some areas, such as where there are wide expanses of surface slickrock, within a few minutes rapid, unseasonal melting can cause flash flooding that is equivalent to heavy local rain.

Flash flooding can be highly destructive and hazardous, but in a land of canyons it is especially violent. Thousands of trickles or streams running harmlessly across open country can join to become a raging torrent in a narrow canyon. Within minutes, normally dry canyon bottoms can run ten feet deep with debris-laden water, and major rivers in the region can double their flow within an hour. Floods funneled through narrow sandstone gorges can wedge great logs between rock walls fifty feet above the gorge floor.

An understanding and respect for this danger is essential for those who explore Canyon Country, whether by vehicle, on horseback or on foot. Most of the time, the region is free of this hazard, but backcountry explorers should be alert for thunderstorms and, when there is snow on the ground, for unseasonally warm winds.

Those who are in hazardous locations when flash flooding threatens should immediately get to higher ground. In canyons, this means moving far above any signs of earlier flooding—plus a little more. Narrow stretches of canyon with sheer walls should always be entered with caution during the thunderstorm season and not entered at all when a rainstorm is predicted or threatening. Experienced Canyon Country explorers know that it is better to play it safe a hundred times than to be caught once by a flash flood.

To avoid the hazards of flash flooding it is necessary to understand and respect them. In Canyon Country, a flash flood can be frightening and destructive, but it can also be a thrilling and unforgettable sight if watched from a safe vantage point.

Flash flood, Seven-Mile Canyon
Tom Till

*"Bloody Mary" in flood,
Arches National Park*
Gerry Wolfe

SEASONS

Even though Canyon Country has a high-desert climate, it still has four distinct seasons, and they vary with elevation. Winter lasts for only two months in most of the region. A storm may pass through in late autumn, but the first real winter weather seldom arrives before mid-December. Winter snows are usually heavy above 8,000 feet, and there is some snow at all elevations every winter. The region's irregular terrain also affects its winter storms. In some of the lower valleys snow generally falls at night, and is rarely accompanied by wind. In lower Moab Valley in southeastern Utah, for example, conventional blizzards simply do not occur.

Winter temperatures in Canyon Country are also fairly mild and vary with elevation. Low-lying rivers in Canyon Country rarely freeze over, although in mid-winter ice does form along their shores. In the deeper parts of the winding Colorado and Green river gorges, ice may bridge short stretches of calm water that the sun does not reach.

Spring arrives early in areas below 6,500 feet, with the first seasonal plants and migrating birds appearing in early March or even sooner. In some Canyon Country valleys, February often brings calm, sunny days and daytime temperatures that are well above freezing. In contrast, the higher roads and trails in Canyon Country mountains may not be passable until June or even July. Below 6,500 feet, the snow is generally gone by March, with little remaining after mid-February except for traces left by occasional brief storms.

Canyon Country weather is generally more variable in the spring than in the winter, with considerable wind and rapid shifts from sunny and warm days to cool, windy, rainy, and overcast weather and then back again, often all within a few hours. For most of the region, spring comes early and lasts only a short time.

Canyon Country can get hot quite early in the year, but its heat is normally desert-dry. Warm weather can begin as early as April, but the real desert heat does not usually begin until late May and it does not persist even then. The region's warmest season generally occurs between mid-June and mid-August, after which late-summer thunder storms break the worst of the summer heat.

September is almost always warm and calm, a long pause between summer and fall. There may be occasional warm days into October, but as the days grow shorter, they also get cooler.

Autumn in Canyon Country is mild and long. Depending on the elevation, the season phases-in during September and may continue well into December. In some protected areas, deciduous foliage may persist into November or even later in some years. Autumn weather is usually calm and sunny, with early-winter storms only rarely upsetting the slow progression into winter. Indian Summer in Canyon Country is often longer than summer itself, and is almost always moderate.

Canyon Country seasons are distinct, but its high-desert climate assures that they will be less extreme than in most of North America.

Cottonwood in Courthouse Wash with Courthouse Towers beyond, Arches National Park
Tom Till

Winter frost, Professor Valley, Utah
F.A. Barnes

Prickly Pear Cactus, Junction Butte, Canyonlands National Park
John P. George

Tamarisk lines the Colorado River near Moab, Utah
F.A. Barnes

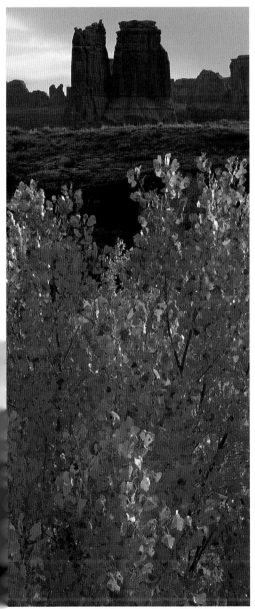

II. HUMAN HISTORY

THE ANCIENT ONES
EARLY EXPLORATION
PIONEERS
SETTLEMENT, GEOGRAPHY AND ECONOMY

Sunrise at Lake Powell,
Glen Canyon National
Recreation Area

Tom Till

THE ANCIENT ONES

Human history in the western hemisphere began during the closing millennia of the great glacial epoch that began some two million years ago and retreated to its present stage around ten thousand years ago. During this long period, so much water was locked into glaciers that the general sea level fell, exposing a strip of land between Alaska and northeastern Asia. As the climate varied, advancing and retreating glaciers exposed the Bering Sea "land bridge" during colder periods. During warmer periods there were relatively ice-free inland corridors from Alaska southward. These two "doors" from Asia to the Americas were opened at the same time for only short intervals.

There is evidence that primitive nomadic Asiatics crossed the Bering Sea land bridge into North America a number of times, probably following the animals they hunted. By about 15,000 years ago, these Asiatics had managed to pass over the land bridge and through the inland ice-free corridors. Older signs of humans have been found in Alaska, but it is doubtful whether these migrants traveled farther south. They probably crossed the land bridge during periods when the inland corridors south were closed.

Once the great northern glaciers began their major retreat, the Bering Sea land bridge closed and the Asiatic migrants were isolated from their homeland. North America was a bounteous land, and as the glaciers retreated, forests rich with animal life developed. The Asians thrived, and

groups moved across North America and southward into South America, adapting to the varied environments and slowly becoming many Indian cultures, the western hemisphere's "Amerind" tribes.

It is not known precisely when the first humans entered the region that we now know as Canyon Country. These early Amerinds were nomadic hunter-gatherers who made no permanent structures and left few durable artifacts. There are positive signs of humans in the region from about five or six thousand years ago, but there are also some indications of earlier use.

It is fairly certain, however, that when humans first arrived in Canyon Country its climate was considerably wetter and cooler than it is now. About 4,000 to 900 years ago when western America was experiencing a mini-glacial period, Canyon Country was doubtless more heavily vegetated, with correspondingly more wildlife. These conditions allowed the nomadic "desert-archaic" tribes of the region to thrive.

About two thousand years ago, Amerind cultures in Canyon Country began to develop a new way of life, probably as a result of ideas and practices brought to the region from the several highly developed Amerind cultures of Central and South America. The major innovation was agriculture and it led to the establishment of permanent communities. Amerind cultures to the north and east of Canyon Country and on the west coast did not make this conversion because they found life much easier than those who

inhabited a land that was slowly but surely growing more arid.

The transition from nomadic life to life in stationary communities based on agriculture permitted the Amerind cultures to develop in Canyon Country. During the next thousand years, they advanced from the Basketmaker stage, with its mud and stick huts, to the Pueblo stage, with its large towns and villages built of native stone.

The Anasazi culture that occupied the southern reaches of Canyon Country and adjoining parts of New Mexico and Nevada developed what eventually became the most sophisticated culture of all North American Indian tribes. The Fremont culture, which occupied northern Canyon Country and much of the present state of Utah, was not quite so advanced in its agriculture, architecture, and trade, but it was exceptional in other ways, such as in its rock graphics.

Beginning about 1200 A.D., the two Amerind cultures in Canyon Country began to abandon the lands they had occupied for centuries. While understanding of this cultural retreat is far from complete, it was probably triggered by a combination of several factors. One was the persistent raiding of the region's peaceful and relatively defenseless agricultural communities by nomadic Indians who had begun to drift into the region. These Indians were the predecessors of the Navajos and Apaches. Another factor was the growing aridity of the land, compounded by consecutive seasons of

PREHISTORIC RUINS

The remains of thousands of prehistoric structures still exist in Canyon Country. Many that were built in open country are discernible only to archaeologists because surface indications have been obscured by nature or destroyed by the "vegetation manipulation" programs that have devastated large areas of pinion-juniper forest over the past decades. But the structures that were built in more protected locations are relatively intact. A few have been excavated, restored to some degree, then stabilized.

Perhaps the most fascinating ruins in Canyon Country are in Mesa Verde National Park in southwestern Colorado, where many cliff dwellings and mesa-top structures are open to the public. Not far away are accessible ruin sites in Hovenweep and Navajo national monuments.

Other accessible prehistoric ruins can be found in Natural Bridges National Monument, Anasazi Indian Village State Historical Monument, and Glen Canyon National Recreation Area. Canyonlands National Park has a number of ruins in its backcountry, and there are many others in unprotected areas adjacent to the park. The canyons and mesas around the Abajo Mountains-Monument Uplift highlands have numerous ruin sites, including Grand Gulch and Montezuma, Arch, White, and Owl Creek- Fish Creek canyons.

Many of the tributary canyons of the Colorado River once had abundant ruins but most of them are now beneath Lake Powell. The remaining few are accessible by boat and a little hiking.

The majority of the prehistoric structures in Canyon Country are remnants of the Anasazi culture. The Fremont culture that once occupied most of the region northwest of the Colorado River left few durable remnants, the most notable of which are numerous exceptional rock art sites in remote locations.

Hovenweep National Monument
Kahnweiler/Johnson

Ruin at Natural Bridges National Monument
Jeff Foott

Wash Ruin
Michael S. Sample

severe drought. Between about 1100 and 1200 A.D., there was a century-long period of exceptional aridity, an interval between mini-glacial periods. A possible third factor was the spread of communicable diseases, perhaps introduced into the region by travelers from Central America, but compounded by growing population density and spread among communities over the existing network of trade routes.

Some groups of Anasazis fled southward where they joined Pueblo tribes in Arizona and New Mexico. Other groups established new settlements where water was more plentiful and in locations that were more easily defended. These survivors of a once thriving culture were still there when the first Spanish explorers entered the region almost three centuries later. The present Hopi, Zuni, and several other Pueblo tribes are believed to be remnants of the Anasazi culture. There is no known relationship between the prehistoric Fremont culture and any modern tribe, and its disappearance remains an archaeological mystery.

From the mid-1200's until white men began to settle in Canyon Country during the late 1800's, the area had no significant Indian population, although hunting parties from surrounding regions did penetrate it, and early American explorers found a few scattered semi-nomadic groups living in the western part of the region.

Mesa Verde National Park
Norman Shrewsbury

ROCK ART

Most of the rock art in Canyon Country has been identified with the two prehistoric Amerind cultures that occupied the region, the Anasazi and Fremont. Some researchers believe that intruders from other regions created a few of the pictograph panels, but there is no proof of this.

"Pictographs" are images painted on rock surfaces using natural pigments. "Petroglyphs" are images pecked or scratched into rock using harder rocks. "Rock art" is generally the term used for both, although it has been established that the prehistoric rock graphics found in Canyon Country have little to do with "art" as that term is presently understood. "Rock graphics" is perhaps a more accurate description.

Because the subject of prehistoric rock graphics is very difficult to study, it is highly controversial; most of the evidence is inferential and there is little opportunity for solid scientific research. There are several techniques for dating other prehistoric artifacts, but none of them work with rock graphics.

Thus, there is little positive, irrefutable knowledge about this fascinating subject and little agreement among researchers. Some claim to be able to "read" prehistoric rock images, calling them "rock writing," and a few profess to see cultural details reflected in rock art images, inferences rejected by others.

There is some evidence, however, indicating how these prehistoric people lived and what was important to their cultures. There are strong indications, for example, that the Anasazi culture possessed some fairly sophisticated astronomical knowledge. Many rock graphic images appear to depict such astronomical events as supernova or are keyed to summer and winter solstices or spring and autumn equinoxes.

Whatever their meaning or purpose, with few exceptions the rock graphics in Canyon Country are crude in both concept and execution. Both the Anasazi and Fremont cultures appear to have been at the very earliest stage of graphics sophistication. Neither, for example, seemed able to depict the third dimension in a two-dimensional image. It is interesting to note that while the Fremont culture seemed to be far less advanced than the Anasazis in other ways, it excelled in rock graphics. Conversely, there are few rock graphics near some of the most highly developed Anasazi communities.

Rock art is abundant in Canyon Country but most of it is in remote locations. Nevertheless, some prehistoric rock art panels are accessible to the general public, and local authorities in the areas listed below are usually willing to provide details and descriptive literature:

UTAH
Arches National Park
Canyonlands National Park
Capitol Reef National Park
Zion National Park
Dinosaur National Monument
   (Utah and Colorado)
Hovenweep National Monument
Natural Bridges National Monument
Newspaper Rock State Historical
   Monument
Grand Gulch Primitive Area
San Rafael Swell
Utah highway 279 (roadside displays)

NEW MEXICO
Bandelier National Monument
Chaco Culture National Historical Park
El Morro National Monument
Three Rivers Petroglyph Site

ARIZONA
Canyon de Chelly National Monument
Navajo National Monument
Petrified Forest National Park

COLORADO
Mesa Verde National Park
Colorado National Monument

NEVADA
Red Rock Canyon
Valley of Fire State Park

All remnants of prehistoric cultures on public land, including rock graphics, are protected by both federal and state laws.

ANTIQUITIES LAWS

Ruins and artifacts are the only remaining sources of information that can tell us about previous inhabitants of Canyon Country. All or part of the scientific value of these cultural resources is destroyed when people disturb ruins, deface rock art and collect pot shards or arrowheads.

There are serious penalties for the theft or vandalism of archaeological or historical resources on federal lands. Under the Archaeological Resources Protection Act of 1979, first-time offenders can be fined up to $20,000 or imprisoned for up to two years, or both. Even though there is a shortage of personnel to thoroughly enforce the law, several offenders have been convicted and given substantial punishments.

Other laws protecting cultural resources are the Antiquities Act of 1906 and the Federal Land Policy and Management Act of 1976. These laws emphasize that cultural resources on federal lands are not to be vandalized, and that they are to be collected only by institutions holding special permits.

Most of the cultural resources in Canyon Country are protected under federal law, since most of the region is federal land managed by the National Park Service, the U. S. Forest Service, and the U. S. Bureau of Land Management. Cultural resources on state lands are protected by state statutes similar to federal laws. Cultural resources on private lands are the property of the private landowner, and under current law they receive no protection except some minimal restrictions for those sites listed on the National Register of Historic Places.

The federal laws protecting cultural resources also apply to some extent to paleontological resources (fossils). Some common fossils, such as petrified wood, may be collected in limited amounts, but less common, more scientifically valuable fossils, such as intact dinosaur bones, may not be collected.

No fossil collecting of any kind is allowed in national parks or monuments, nor in most state park areas. Local Forest Service and Bureau of Land Management offices have information about what fossils may be collected on their lands.

Moon House, Cedar Mesa, Utah
Tom Bean

EARLY EXPLORATION

Early Spanish explorers traveled through the outer reaches of Canyon Country in the sixteenth century, but they did not enter the region itself until much later. In 1540, Coronado crossed what is now central Arizona and New Mexico and encountered remnants of the Anasazi culture as well as other Indian tribes before continuing eastward. During the next two centuries, other Spanish and Mexican explorers ventured into the Southwest but they did not enter Canyon Country proper.

In 1776, the Dominguez-Escalante expedition set out to find a route between Spanish settlements in Santa Fe and southern California. The expedition failed in this objective, but its looping route touched the eastern part of Canyon Country and briefly re-entered the region in the southwest to cross the Colorado River upriver of present-day Glen Canyon Dam. This historic "Crossing of the Fathers," which was later used by other explorers, is now inundated by Lake Powell.

During the early 1800's, a few Spanish, Mexican, and American explorers traveled into Canyon Country seeking practical trade routes across this unexplored part of the continent. Eventually, they established a route that became known as the Old Spanish Trail. This trade route between New Mexico and California passed within the border-lands of Canyon Country and was used from 1829 until 1848 when the western territories were acquired from Mexico and American explorers established better routes west. During this same period fur trappers entered Canyon Country via its rivers,

leaving little record of their explorations other than the few inscriptions they carved into sandstone cliffs and boulders.

Shortly after the United States acquired the western territories from Mexico, several surveys were made seeking possible wagon and railroad routes that could link the eastern states with the West Coast. One of these routes crossed Canyon Country's northern borderlands. In 1859, a Topographical Engineers exploring party followed the Old Spanish Trail route from Santa Fe into what is now southeastern Utah.

Professor John S. Newberry made the first documented description of southeastern Utah and what is now Canyonlands National Park. Newberry was general scientist for the 1859 Macomb Expedition, a military survey party charged with mapping the region, noting valuable minerals and other potentially useful information, and ultimately reaching the confluence of the Green and Colorado rivers. The expedition was to follow the Old Spanish Trail into eastern Utah and then return to Santa Fe by way of a more southerly route along the San Juan River.

The expedition completed its tasks, although their reported sighting of the confluence was erroneous, but the outbreak of the Civil War delayed the release of the expedition report. By the time it was published seventeen years later, so much information had been lost that historians have had difficulty piecing the entire story together. Recent field and archive research, however, has discovered many missing details including the route taken by

J.S. Newberry sketch of Six-shooter Peaks from Macomb Expedition Report

Above left: Abandoned pioneer ranch, Unaweep Canyon, Colorado
F.A. Barnes

Above right: Ekker Ranch at Robber's Roost, Wayne County, Utah
Rodney Greeno

Below left: Bluff Cemetery
Scott S. Warren

Below right: Old Homestead, Salt Creek, Canyonlands National Park
Joe Arnold, Jr.

OUTLAWS

The history and legends of outlaws in Canyon Country are as rich as those of any region in the West. The names of the robbers and rustlers who spent much of their careers in Canyon Country form a Who's Who of outlawry: Robert LeRoy Parker (Butch Cassidy), Harry Longabaugh (the Sundance Kid), Harvey Logan (Kid Curry), Matt Warner, Tom and Bill McCarty, Elzy Lay, Ben Kilpatrick, Mike Cassidy, George (Flat Nose) Curry, and dozens of others who were more or less associated with Butch Cassidy's "Wild Bunch." During the 1880's and 1890's these men robbed banks, stole horses, and rustled cattle throughout the West; they seldom suffered the consequences.

One of the Wild Bunch's principal hideouts, Robbers Roost, was in the heart of Canyon Country near the western boundary of today's Canyonlands National Park. Robbers Roost had water, grass for livestock, and defensible approaches. Hanksville, the nearest settlement, provided supplies with few questions. Butch Cassidy was well-liked in the area as the gentleman bandit who supposedly never killed anyone, and fear of retribution must have enhanced the lawabiders willingness to cooperate with the group.

The Wild Bunch committed all of their major robberies outside Canyon Country and retreated to the canyons between robberies. After robbing a bank in Telluride, Colorado on June 24, 1889, Butch Cassidy, Tom McCarty and Matt Warner fled to the canyons of eastern Utah, crossing the Colorado River at Moab and traveling north to Browns Hole on the Green River near Vernal, Utah. Other Wild Bunch robberies on the fringes of Canyon Country included the McCarty brothers' bank robbery in Delta, Colorado, on September 7, 1893, and Butch Cassidy's payroll robbery at Castle Gate, Utah, on April 21, 1897.

Few attempted to capture members of the Wild Bunch. The dangers of ambush in the rugged canyons and the lack of cooperation from the locals kept most lawmen from pursuing the outlaws. At the turn of the century, however, Sheriff Preece of Vernal and Sheriff Tyler of Moab followed rustlers into the Book Cliffs and the San Rafael Swell. While searching for a rustler whom the sheriff in Price would not arrest, Tyler killed "Flat Nose" George Curry in a shootout on the Green River. Tyler promptly paid the ultimate price for his courage and indiscretion in a surprise attack by outlaws in the Book Cliffs. His murderers were never captured.

The Wild Bunch successfully eluded the law but when their leader, Butch Cassidy, left for South America, the group broke up, leaving little evidence of its existence beyond corrals and inscriptions at Robbers Roost and other remote locations in Canyon Country.

Above: Butch Cassidy and his gang in 1900. Left to right: Harry Longabaugh, Bill Carver, Ben Kilpatrick, Harvey Logan and Robert Parker, alias Butch Cassidy
Utah State Historical Society

Below left: Elza Lay, outlaw
Utah State Historical Society

Below right: Harvey Logan, outlaw
Utah State Historical Society

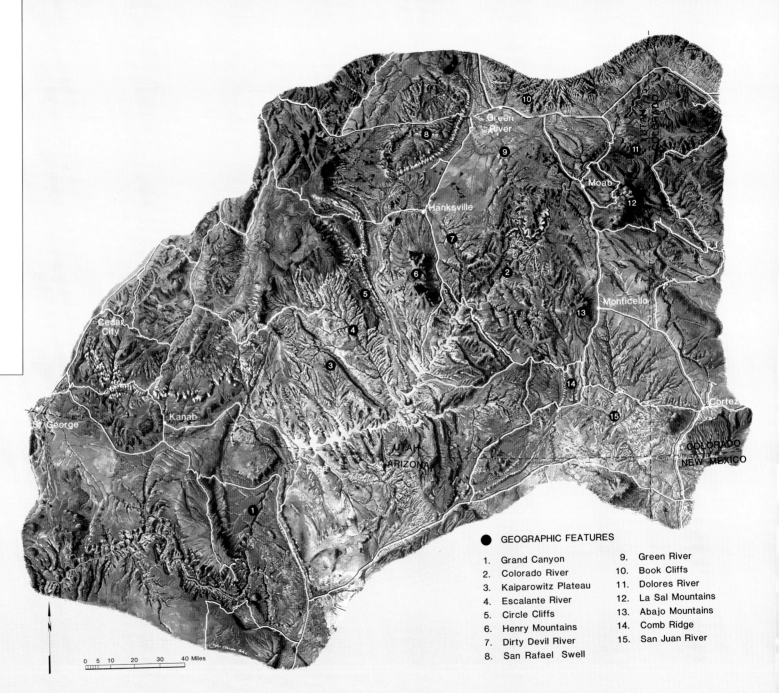

CANYONS OF THE COLORADO RIVER

This stereographic map encompasses the Colorado Plateau and graphically represents the landforms carved by the Colorado River and its tributaries.

This version of the map is a minor adaptation of a map which was conceived and designed by Lin Ottinger of Moab, Utah, and drawn by French artist Jean-Claud Gal. *Canyons of the Colorado* is available in a 24" x 34" color format from Lin Ottinger Tours, 137 North Main, Moab, Utah 84532.

© Lin Ottinger Tours, 1984. Used by permission.

● GEOGRAPHIC FEATURES

1. Grand Canyon
2. Colorado River
3. Kaiparowitz Plateau
4. Escalante River
5. Circle Cliffs
6. Henry Mountains
7. Dirty Devil River
8. San Rafael Swell
9. Green River
10. Book Cliffs
11. Dolores River
12. La Sal Mountains
13. Abajo Mountains
14. Comb Ridge
15. San Juan River

0 5 10 20 30 40 Miles

SETTLEMENT

Even during its several mineral boom periods, the population of Canyon Country has probably never exceeded 50,000 people. The arid heartland of Canyon Country has always been sparsely populated and perhaps three-quarters of its permanent occupants live within the region's more hospitable borderlands. The principal towns in Canyon Country are Green River, Moab, Monticello, Blanding, and Kanab in Utah, Cortez in Colorado, and Page in Arizona. Except for Page, none of these towns has a population of more than 7,000 people and most have less than half of that.

There are a number of even smaller communities including Bluff, Mexican Hat, Thompson, Hanksville, La Sal, Torrey, Boulder, Escalante, Tropic, Henrieville, and Cannonville in Utah, and Gateway and Paradox in Colorado. Several small communities are located near the marinas that serve Lake Powell, and others lie within the Navajo Indian Reservation, on the Utah-Arizona border in Monument Valley and at Kayenta.

The largest cities on the borders of Canyon Country are St. George, Cedar City, and Price, Utah, and Grand Junction, Colorado. These communities and the large urban areas of north- central Utah provide services for Canyon Country residents that its own, more limited, commercial enterprises cannot offer.

GHOST TOWNS

Canyon Country's spectacular natural attractions are complemented by the fascinating historic remnants of failed or forgotten human ventures. These historic attractions range from flooded-out Mormon farming settlements to ill-conceived isolated ranchsteads, ephemeral mining boom towns, and even a religious zealot's too-good-to-last colony. All provide glimpses into the lives of those who faced this land on its harsh terms.

The abandoned Mormon farming settlements are among the more interesting and well-preserved ghost towns of Canyon Country. Most of these towns are located along the Virgin River below Zion National Park, along Johnson Creek and the Paria River near Kanab, in the lower Fremont River valley near Capitol Reef National Park, and in Castle Valley near Castle Dale.

Grafton, on the Virgin River, is possibly the most picturesque ghost town in Utah, with a school and church still standing and a cemetery below the dramatic cliffs of Zion National Park. Grafton was settled during the 1860's and survived nearly to the turn of the century when repeated floods eventually drove the settlers out.

Old Paria, forty miles east of Kanab, was also settled in the 1860's. Floods and droughts finally caused the town to die out near the turn of the century. There are still several pioneer houses, foundations, corrals, and a cemetery at Old Paria. Nearby is a western movie set built in 1963. There are a few other ghost towns with standing structures near Kanab, including Adairville, Johnson and Upper Kanab.

The lower Fremont Valley, between Capitol Reef National Park and Hanksville, contains at least six ghost towns that were established during the 1880's and had failed by 1910 because of repeated floods. There are a few houses and a church-schoolhouse at Caineville, and two houses, some foundations, and walls at Giles.

The Capitol Reef visitor center and campground are located near the old town of Fruita. Extensive fruit tree orchards and several structures remain here. Today the area is managed by the National Park Service as an historic resource for the benefit of park visitors.

Desert Lake and Victor, twenty miles northeast of Castle Dale, both lacked suitable farmland to survive for more than a decade or so. Some houses and other buildings from the 1880's and 1890's still stand.

Although there have been several mining booms, there are few substantial mining ghost towns in Canyon Country. One of the most picturesque is Temple Mountain in the San Rafael Swell near Goblin Valley State Reserve. Temple Mountain was the site of two uranium booms, the first just before and during World War I, when uranium oxide was mined for use in paints and ceramic glazes, and the second during the 1950's. A few rock houses remain from the first boom and some mine works from the second boom. A coal-mining ghost town is located about five miles north of Thompson, Utah, at Sego, where several rock buildings, some walls and a cemetery remain. The western Colorado portion of Canyon Country has few ghost towns except for some partially abandoned mining set-tlements, such as Gateway on the Dolores River.

A few stereotypical western mining boom towns were built in Canyon Country, including Miners Basin in the La Sal Mountains near Moab and Eagle City in the Henry Mountains near Hanksville. Both towns were based on gold and silver mines in the 1890's and early 1900's and had saloons, stores, and hotels. Little remains of Eagle City, but some of the remnants of the Miners Basin settlement are still visible in a dense growth of trees.

One of the strangest and still largely intact ghost towns in Canyon Country is the Home of Truth Colony fifteen miles north of Monticello on Utah 211. Marie Ogden founded the Colony in 1933 as a communal stronghold in which to survive the destruction that she believed would soon visit the Earth. One of Ogden's bizarre activities was an attempt to resurrect a corpse. Her followers, who had given up their personal belongings when they joined the colony, departed with nothing to their names as the sheriff arrived.

Remnants of abandoned ranches can be found throughout Canyon Country in remote, seldom-visited locations. Two of the best known are Wolfe Ranch (previously known as Turnbow Cabin) in Arches National Park and Starr Ranch at Starr Springs Campground, forty miles south of Hanksville. There are many other abandoned ranches at the ends of jeep trails, on remote river banks, and in stands of trees, offering diversions to modern explorers who happen across them.

GEOGRAPHY

As pioneer settlers headed west from the more populous eastern and midwestern states to the newly acquired western territories, various federal laws allowed them to claim public land. The Homestead Act permitted settlers to obtain ownership of blocks of land by occupying and farming them; the Desert Entry Act granted much the same privilege but did not require the settler to live on the land; and the 1872 Mining Act encouraged the development of mineral claims and conveyed to claimants actual ownership of land that had proven mineral value.

During the 19th and most of the 20th Centuries, government policy was to give federally owned public land to almost anyone who could find an economic use for it. As each western state was established, it was given large blocks of land, some of it consolidated around existing developments and some of it in scattered, mile-square "sections." Many of these sections of state land still remain isolated inside vast tracts of federal land. The concept of permanent government ownership of the remaining federal public land did not become law until 1976, although a few areas were preserved within the nation's growing National Park system beginning in 1872, and other areas were designated National Forests after 1905.

Most of Canyon Country, however, was considered to be too worthless to claim even though vast expanses of its forest lands and even arid desert lands were leased for livestock grazing. As a result, about 90 percent of Canyon Country is still in federal ownership. The U.S. Forest Service, the Bureau of Land Management, and the National Park Service administer most of the region. The Bureau of Indian Affairs has jurisdiction over the Indian reservations. Although these federal agencies encourage the development of mineral, water, timber, and grazing resources on all but Park Service lands, current national policy is to retain permanent public ownership of most federal land.

Canyon Country's surface geography, its general aridity, and the predominance of public land have established limits to the region's conventional development. The Colorado River slashes diagonally across the center of Canyon Country where it is joined by other rivers such as the Green and San Juan. All have created deep, sheer-walled gorges within the ancient sandstone landscape, as have many of their tributaries such as the Dolores, San Rafael, Dirty Devil, Escalante, Paria, and Virgin rivers. Even the region's numerous perennial and seasonal streams have carved deep canyons over the last few million years.

High mesa farming above
Hovenweep Canyon
Paul Logsdon

Opposite right: Atlas Minerals
Corporation tailings pond,
Moab, Utah
Paul Logsdon

ECONOMY

Above this immense and complex maze of canyons, sprawling deserts, arid plains, and broken reefs, still more ridges and bluffs of colorful sandstone dominate the landscape. One early military explorer reported that this stupendous land of canyons was "worthless and impracticable." This opinion dominated public thinking until the early 1900's, when commercial quantities of several minerals were discovered in the region. Oil and gas were found and developed in Canyon Country's southeastern corner, coal was found at several places in the region's newer geologic deposits, and three other valuable minerals were discovered.

The first of these was radium, which was used for medical purposes and for research into the nature of radioactive elements. Vanadium was mined next and used in the high-strength steels needed during World Wars I and II. Uranium, the last mineral to be developed, is still being taken from the region but its mining, milling, and use have been cyclic due to political and economic factors.

Although the population of Canyon Country has tended to grow and dwindle in reaction to mining activity, the region has always had an economy based on farming and livestock. Shortly after the turn of the century, tourism and recreation began adding to the economy. In recent years, many Americans from outside the region have discovered that certain areas in Canyon Country are ideal for retirement living. Seasonal hunting and fishing by non-resident sportsmen have also contributed to a more stable economic base.

A Navajo woman ties her companion's hair in a traditional chongo
Stewart Atchison

Navajo children of Monument Valley in traditional dress
Stewart Aitchison

While the vast majority of Canyon Country is "worthless" for any conventional economic purpose other than marginal livestock grazing, a few of its valleys have bloomed as their water resources have been developed. Since its early years, Moab Valley in southeastern Utah and several other areas to the west have had bountiful groves of fruit trees. The historic settlement of Fruita, now within Capitol Reef National Park, was named after its thriving groves of apples, pears, peaches, cherries, plums, and apricots. Farmers in certain areas, such as Green River, Utah, grow exceptionally tasty melons. With irrigation, many of the region's river and stream bottomlands and alluvial benches are excellent places to grow alfalfa and even some grains.

The three Indian reservations that occupy areas of Canyon Country also contribute to the region's economy from incomes outside the region, from tourism, and from mineral developments within reservations. The small Kaibab Indian Reservation is in the western tip of Canyon Country, and some of the Ute Mountain Indian Reservation occupies its southeastern corner. Part of the immense Navajo Indian Reservation occupies the entire area to the south of the Colorado and San Juan rivers plus a small area to the north of the San Juan in the vicinity of Aneth and Montezuma Creek.

Development of limited water resources has been vital to the region's agriculture and its need for domestic water. Except for water used in the vicinity of Page, which comes from Lake Powell, communities in Canyon Country use very little water directly from the Colorado River. Many small rivers and tributary streams are diverted for irrigation (and are thus withheld from the Colorado), and a large amount of water is pumped from ancient underground aquifers.

Several areas within Canyon Country also use water from nearby highlands that receive more precipitation than the lower country. Moab Valley obtains all of its domestic and agricultural water either from surface streams that originate within the nearby La Sal Mountains or from wells that tap aquifers that are replenished from the same source.

Settlements and ranches at the base of the Abajo Mountains use surface and subsurface waters that originate in the mountains, and others use water from the lofty Aquarius Plateau in the Boulder, Escalante, Grover, Torrey, and Teasdale areas. Other highlands in the High Plateau region provide water for communities in the western tip of Canyon Country. Water users in the Hanksville area tap streams and aquifers that originate in the Henry Mountains, but they also draw water from the nearby Fremont and Muddy rivers.

The Fremont flows from mountainous highlands northwest of Capitol Reef National Park and joins the Muddy to form the Dirty Devil. The Muddy originates in the lofty interior of the San Rafael Swell.

There is a surprising amount of water available for use in Canyon Country, most of it from reliable sources that vary little from year to year. In the future, however, this water may have to be used more efficiently if the region's economy is to thrive.

III. SPECIAL AREAS

Queen's Garden from
Sunset Point, Bryce
Canyon National Park
Jeff Gnass

NATIONAL PARKS
NATIONAL MONUMENTS
GLEN CANYON NATIONAL RECREATION AREA
STATE PARKS, BLM AREAS AND WILDERNESS

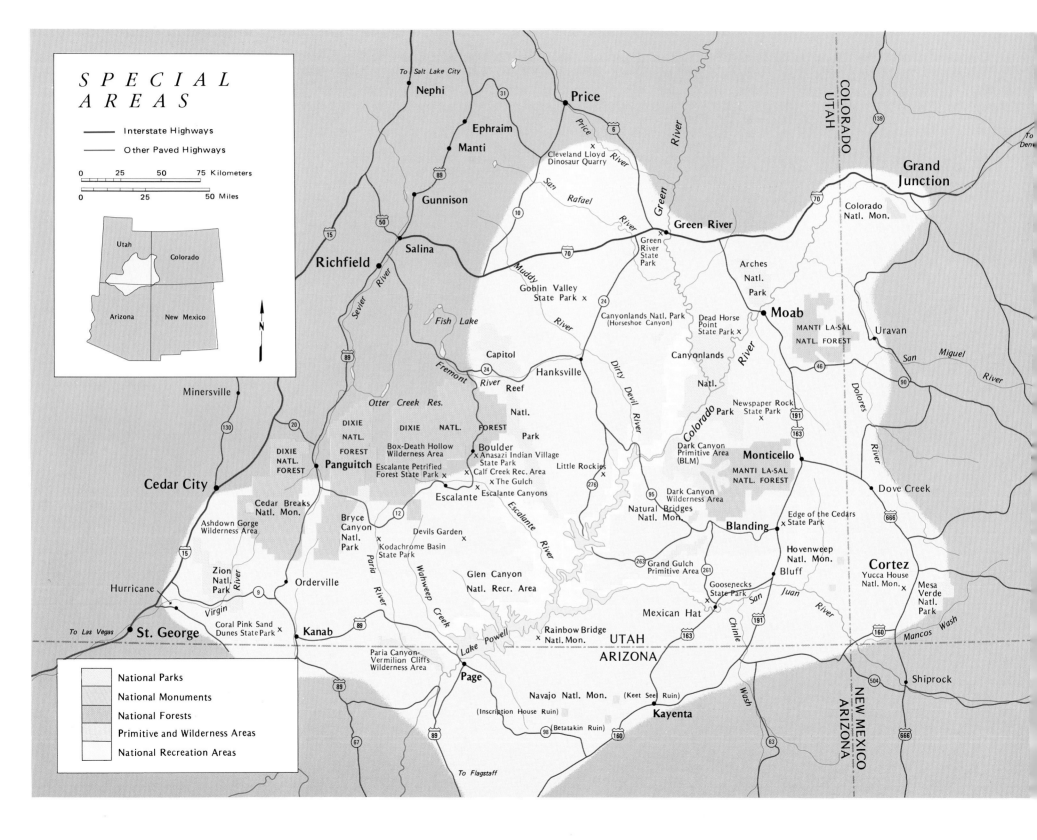

SPECIAL AREAS

— Interstate Highways
— Other Paved Highways

0 25 50 75 Kilometers
0 25 50 Miles

Utah
Colorado
Arizona
New Mexico

N

National Parks
National Monuments
National Forests
Primitive and Wilderness Areas
National Recreation Areas

To Salt Lake City
Nephi
Price
COLORADO
UTAH
Grand Junction
Ephraim
Manti
Cleveland Lloyd x
Dinosaur Quarry
Price River
Green River
Gunnison
San Rafael
Green River
Green River State Park
Colorado Natl. Mon.
Salina
Richfield
Muddy River
Goblin Valley State Park x
Arches Natl. Park
Moab
MANTI LA-SAL NATL. FOREST
Uravan
Sevier River
Fish Lake
Canyonlands Natl. Park (Horseshoe Canyon)
Dead Horse Point State Park x
San Miguel River
Minersville
Otter Creek Res.
Capitol
Hanksville
Reef
Canyonlands
Colorado River
Natl.
Newspaper Rock State Park x
DIXIE NATL. FOREST
Fremont River
Natl.
Dirty Devil River
Park
Dark Canyon Primitive Area (BLM)
Monticello
DIXIE NATL. FOREST
DIXIE NATL. FOREST
Box-Death Hollow Wilderness Area
Boulder
x Anasazi Indian Village State Park
Little Rockies x
MANTI LA-SAL NATL. FOREST
Panguitch
Escalante Petrified Forest State Park x
Calf Creek Rec. Area
x The Gulch
Escalante Canyons
Dark Canyon Wilderness Area
Natural Bridges Natl. Mon.
Edge of the Cedars x State Park
Dove Creek
Cedar City
Cedar Breaks Natl. Mon.
Escalante
Escalante River
Blanding
Ashdown Gorge Wilderness Area
Bryce Canyon Natl. Park
Devils Garden x
Hovenweep Natl. Mon.
Cortez
Zion Natl. Park
Kodachrome Basin State Park
Glen Canyon Natl. Recr. Area
Grand Gulch Primitive Area
Bluff
Yucca House Natl. Mon. x
Mesa Verde Natl. Park
Hurricane
Virgin River
Orderville
Paria River
Goosenecks State Park
Mexican Hat
San Juan River
To Las Vegas
St. George
Coral Pink Sand Dunes State Park x
Kanab
Wahweep Creek
Rainbow Bridge x Natl. Mon.
UTAH
ARIZONA
Chinle
Shiprock
Paria Canyon-Vermilion Cliffs Wilderness Area
Lake Powell
Page
Navajo Natl. Mon.
(Keet Seel Ruin)
NEW MEXICO
ARIZONA
(Inscription House Ruin)
Kayenta
To Flagstaff
(Betatakin Ruin)

NATIONAL PARKS

Canyon Country has the greatest concentration in the nation of areas administered by the National Park Service. The region is so unique, however, that it contains many other large areas that, had they been located anywhere else in the country, would now be protected within the National Park system. Within Canyon Country some local resistance to the establishment of National Parks and Monuments may have limited their size and slowed the upgrading of some National Monuments to National Park status.

Despite this opposition, Canyon Country has six National Parks within its borders: Arches, Canyonlands, and Mesa Verde in the east, Capitol Reef in the center, and Bryce and Zion in the west. Each of these parks contains a wide variety of spectacular land forms, unusual flora and fauna, and fascinating remnants of human history. All six offer easy access to fair samplings of their special features, and all contain primitive areas that offer visitors the chance to enjoy unbroken solitude in completely natural settings.

Arches National Park was established as a National Monument in 1929, with two separate sections called The Devils Garden and The Windows. The Monument's boundaries were adjusted in 1938, 1960 and 1969. It was granted National Park status in 1971.

Arches National Park was named for the astonishing number and variety of natural arches that have formed within its maze of spectacular sandstone outcroppings. These "fins" and "domes" were produced when a long ridge of salt deep beneath the surface thrust overlying rock layers upward, tilting and cracking them. Millions of years of erosion subsequently exposed the fractured sandstone, allowing rain and seeping water to carve it into the present fantasyland of red-hued sandstone shapes and slowly forming hundreds of natural arches.

A paved road with several spurs and numerous scenic pullouts penetrates the park. Hiking trails provide access to many of the park's natural arches, and other arches are accessible by hiking into primitive areas. Arches is one of the few areas administered by the National Park Service with four-wheel drive trails which permit access to areas that would otherwise be difficult to reach.

The only overnight facilities in the park are developed campsites near the end of the main paved road, but a variety of commercial accommodations are available in the nearby town of Moab. The park is open to the public year around, and its main road is rarely closed by winter snow.

Bryce Canyon National Park was initially established as a National Monument in 1923. It was redesignated Utah National Park the following year and then renamed Bryce Canyon National Park in 1928. Its boundaries were adjusted later in 1928, in 1930, three times in 1931, and again in 1942. Bryce is essentially a long bluff that is heavily forested on top. Below the bluff's rim, highly mineralized Cretaceous lake-bed sediments have eroded into a vividly colorful complex of towers, spires, and ridges. Rain erosion has created numerous natural arches and windows within these strange forms.

Access to the park is by a paved road that winds through the forestland on top of the park's elevated bluff. At numerous pullouts, park visitors can experience panoramic views of the vividly colorful, wildly eroded sediments below the rim. Established hiking trails that follow isolated stretches of this rim and enter the maze below permit a closer appreciation of the park's unusual beauty.

Campgrounds and commercial accommodations are available within and adjacent to Bryce Canyon National Park and in the nearby town of Panguitch. During the winter, parts of the park become inaccessible because of heavy snow, but the main viewpoints are kept open.

Canyonlands National Park was established in 1964 and expanded in 1971. The immense park contains four distinct geographic areas and a separate annex. The areas are defined by surface geology and the Green and Colorado rivers, which join within the park.

The rivers and their spectacular inner gorges are at the heart of Canyonlands. In the north, the Island-in-the-Sky is a convoluted, sheer-walled mesa that soars high above the benchlands that rim the inner gorges. To the west of the rivers, tributary canyons have formed The Maze, a gigantic geologic labyrinth. To the southeast of the Colorado River is The Needles with its spectacular slender and colorful sandstone spires. The Horseshoe Canyon annex protects several large panels of prehistoric rock art.

Access to The Needles and Island-in-the-Sky is via paved roads that offer many scenic views. The only access to the interior of The

Maze is by four-wheel drive trails or backpacking. The river gorges can be viewed from vantage points within The Maze and The Needles and from the rim of the Island-in-the-Sky and the White Rim below the Island. Raft trips down the park's rivers permit even closer views of their wild scenic beauty. There are hiking trails throughout the park.

There are developed campgrounds on the Island-in-the-Sky and in The Needles, but only primitive campsites within The Maze, in Horseshoe Canyon, and along the rivers. On the eastern side of the park, commercial accommodations are available in nearby Moab and Monticello, but there are none within practical range of the western part of the park. The park is open year around, but its rivers are generally inaccessible during the winter.

Capitol Reef National Park was established as a National Monument in 1937. Its boundaries were adjusted in 1958, 1969, and again in 1971 when it was given National Park status. As with the other parks within Canyon Country, Capitol Reef was established to protect its outstanding geologic features, in this case a gigantic "monocline" or ridge of tilted and distorted sandstone some seventy miles long. The Fremont River and several of its tributaries cut through this immense ridge which has also been deeply sliced by erosion many other places. The exposed geologic strata on both flanks of the monocline have eroded into brilliantly colorful fantasyland shapes.

A paved Utah state highway goes through the park and closely parallel to the scenic Fremont River, and a good graded road allows access to one of the most spectacular stretches of the Reef. Four-wheel drive trails penetrate the park's backcountry, as do a number of established hiking trails. Backpacking into the park's wilderness areas is permitted.

There is a developed campground within Capitol Reef near park headquarters, and primitive camping is permitted in the backcountry. The nearest commercial accommodations are in Hanksville to the east and Torrey to the west. The park is open year around.

Mesa Verde National Park was established in 1906 in response to public outrage over collectors looting great quantities of artifacts from the area's extensive pre-Columbian cliff dwellings. Its boundaries were adjusted in 1913, 1931, 1932, and 1963. Although the setting of Mesa Verde is wooded mesas and deep sandstone canyons, the park was established primarily to protect its extensive prehistoric ruins rather than its natural values.

Access to Mesa Verde is by paved park road from the main highway between Cortez and Durango, in the southwestern corner of Colorado. Within the park, access to the ruins and other points of interest on one elevated peninsula is by paved road. Special buses take visitors to a more isolated area of the park, and the park has numerous hiking trails.

There is a campground in the park and commercial lodging is available in the park and in nearby Cortez and Durango. Mesa Verde is open year around, but since most of it lies between 7,000 and 8,000 feet the roads are often closed by snow during the winter. Park-operated facilities and services are available from about mid-May through mid-October. Concession facilities are open from about mid-April through mid-November.

Zion National Park was first established in 1909 as Mukuntuweep National Monument. In 1918, its boundaries were adjusted and its name changed to Zion National Monument. The Monument was given National Park status the following year, and its boundary was again changed in 1930. In 1956, an addition made to the Monument in 1937 was incorporated into the Park. Another boundary adjustment was made in 1960.

Zion is a land of stupendous canyons cut into ancient sandstone formations. In the main body of the park, the cutting has been done by the Virgin River and its tributaries, with other streams sculpturing outlying areas of the park.

The lower part of Zion Canyon is accessible by paved road. A paved spur road connects from the east, and two others enter western areas of the park. Established hiking trails and routes allow access to the park's extensive backcountry.

There are both public campgrounds and commercial accommodations within the park as well as other overnight facilities in Springdale at the park entrance and in small towns nearby. Cedar City to the north and St. George to the southwest are the nearest cities. The park is open year around although much of its backcountry is inaccessible during the winter.

NOTES:

1. This generalized stratigraphic chart shows the relative ages and relationships of the geologic strata exposed on the surface within the six national parks in Canyon Country.

2. The contour lines on the left side of each column indicate the approximate slope each geologic stratum takes when its edge is exposed by erosion.

3. In this chart, the geologic strata common to two or more parks are shown to be equal in depth. In fact, they vary considerably from park to park, and within each park.

Chart data compiled by F. A. Barnes based on reports published by the U.S. Geological Survey and the Four Corners Geological Society. Photos, left to right, F.A. Barnes, F.A. Barnes, F.A. Barnes, F.A. Barnes, Tom Till, F.A. Barnes.

ZION NATIONAL PARK
UTAH

CANYONLANDS NATIONAL PARK
UTAH

MILLION YEARS AGO	GEOLOGIC TIME PERIODS	GEOLOGIC FORMATIONS COMMON TO TWO OR MORE NATIONAL PARKS
	TERTIARY	
65		
	CRETACEOUS	
		Mancos Shale
		Dakota Sandstone
136		Morrison Formation
		Summerville Formation
		Curtis Formation
	JURASSIC	Entrada Sandstone
		Carmel Formation
		Navajo Sandstone
190		
		Kayenta Formation
	TRIASSIC	Wingate Sandstone
		Chinle Formation
		Moenkopi Formation
225		
	PERMIAN	
280		
	PENNSYLVANIAN	

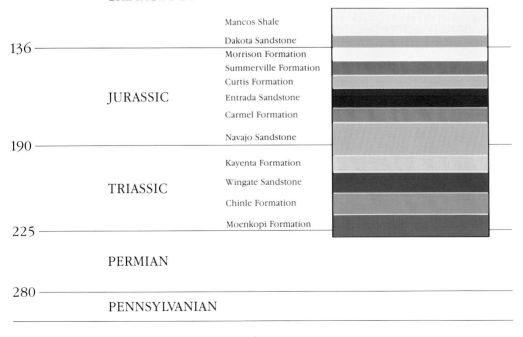

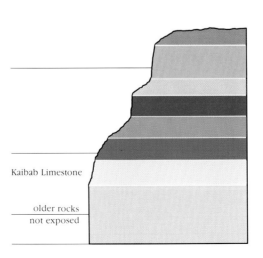

Kaibab Limestone

older rocks
not exposed

Cutler Formation

Honaker Trail Formation

older rocks not
exposed

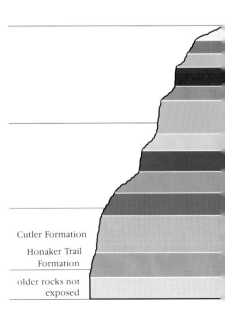

CHES NATIONAL PARK
H

CAPITOL REEF NATIONAL PARK
UTAH

MESA VERDE NATIONAL PARK
COLORADO

BRYCE CANYON NATIONAL PARK
UTAH

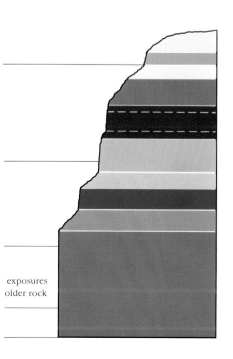

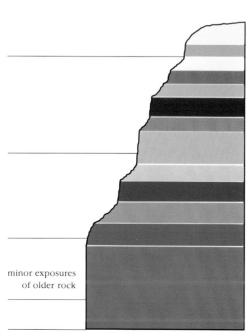

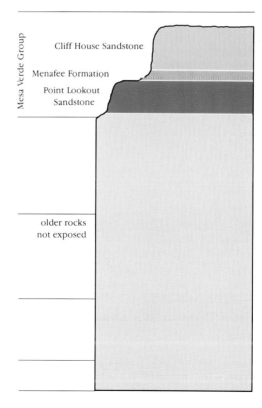

Mesa Verde Group

Cliff House Sandstone

Menafee Formation

Point Lookout
Sandstone

older rocks
not exposed

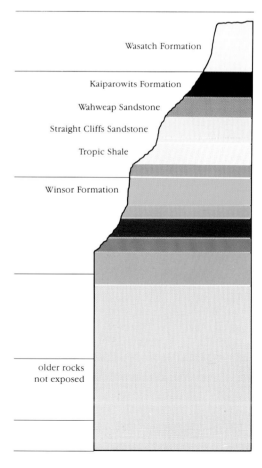

Wasatch Formation

Kaiparowits Formation

Wahweap Sandstone

Straight Cliffs Sandstone

Tropic Shale

Winsor Formation

older rocks
not exposed

exposures
older rock

minor exposures
of older rock

NATIONAL MONUMENTS

Hovenweep National Monument in southeastern Utah was established in 1923 to protect six isolated prehistoric ruin sites. The monument headquarters and one ruin site in Utah are accessible by graded road, but other ruins are on both sides of the nearby Colorado-Utah state line.

Natural Bridges National Monument, also in southeastern Utah, was established in 1908 to protect three immense natural bridges and the surrounding area. Pullouts along a paved road provide views of the bridges and access to hiking trails that go beneath them.

Rainbow Bridge National Monument, in southcentral Utah, was established in 1910 to protect this immense and spectacularly beautiful natural span. It is accessible either by boat on Lake Powell or by horse trail from a remote Navajo trading post.

Cedar Breaks National Monument, in southwestern Utah, was established in 1933 to protect erosional landforms similar to those in Bryce Canyon National Park. Pullouts along a paved road provide views of a huge amphitheater filled with pastel-hued pinnacles, towers, and ridges.

Colorado National Monument was established in 1911 to protect an enormous bluff of red-hued sandstone that looms high above the Colorado River near Grand Junction, Colorado. A paved road along the rim of this bluff provides spectacular views of the river valley far below.

Yucca House is a little-known National Monument established by presidential proclamation in 1919 to protect Anasazi ruins south of Cortez, Colorado. It is not open to the public.

Navajo National Monument in northern Arizona was set aside in 1909 to protect several outstanding prehistoric cliff-dwelling ruins. A paved road goes to the Monument headquarters and a museum, but the ruins are accessible only by ranger-guided hiking tours.

Pipe Spring National Monument, also in northern Arizona, was established in 1923 to preserve the remains of a pioneer Mormon fort and settlement. It is accessible by paved road.

Armstrong Canyon, Natural Bridges National Monument
Gerry Wolfe

GLEN CANYON NATIONAL RECREATION AREA

Glen Canyon National Recreation Area, the largest federal park area in Canyon Country, was established following the completion of Glen Canyon Dam in 1964. The area includes Lake Powell, much of the lower Escalante River canyon system, and a northern arm adjacent to Canyonlands National Park. The region to the south of lower Lake Powell and its San Juan River arm is in the Navajo Indian Reservation. Within the recreation area, the canyon system of the Colorado River and its tributaries is uniquely spectacular.

Lake Powell is accessible at four developed marinas, and others are being planned. Paved roads cross the Colorado River gorge just below the dam, cross the lake near its upper end, and reach the lake at two points about 100 miles uplake from the dam. Power boats are necessary for extensive travel on this 180-mile-long desert lake. Hiking from the lake provides the only access to much of the recreation area's backcountry, although some areas are accessible by off-road vehicles on trails that branch from paved perimeter roads.

Each marina on Lake Powell has a developed campground, and primitive camping from boats is also permitted. Commercial accommodations are only available near the marinas and at the town of Page near the dam. The recreation area is open year around.

Wahweap Marina on Lake Powell, Glen Canyon National Recreation Area
Jeff Gnass

WHICH ARCH IS THE BIGGEST?

Finding the answer to the question, "Which arch in Canyon Country is biggest?", depends on how "size" is defined and how measurements are made. A span's size is usually determined by the maximum width of its opening, but spans in Canyon Country have varied shapes, making comparisons awkward. Measuring techniques also vary, further complicating the matter.

Even though a precise answer to the size question cannot be provided, existing measurements give some indication of the sizes of the largest natural spans in the region.

By almost any method of measuring, the two largest spans are Landscape Arch in Arches National Park and Kolob Arch in Zion National Park. Each arch has been carefully measured by two scientific teams; each team has designated a different winner in the size contest; and each is correct within the context of its definitions and techniques.

There are dozens of natural spans in the 100 to 200-foot range, but there are only nine with openings exceeding 200 feet in one dimension. These spans

are listed below with their current official measurements. All are in Utah except Wrather Arch, which is in northern Arizona. The paired figures given for Kolob and Landscape are those of the two scientific teams that measured them in 1984.

	span in feet
Kolob Arch, Zion National Park	310/292
Landscape Arch, Arches National Park	291/306
Rainbow Bridge, Rainbow Bridge National Monument	275
Sipapu Natural Bridge, Natural Bridges N.M.	261
Morning Glory Arch, Negro Bill Canyon	243
Stevens Arch, Glen Canyon N.R.A.	225
Kachina Natural Bridge, Natural Bridges N.M.	206
Owachomo Natural Bridge, Natural Bridges N.M.	200
Wrather Arch, Paria Canyon Wilderness Area	200

Landscape Arch, Arches National Park

Michael S. Sample

STATE PARKS

There are a number of Canyon Country areas which are administered by the Utah State Division of Parks and Recreation. All are readily accessible and most have developed visitor facilities. In the past, these areas were variously designated as state parks, state reserves and state historical monuments, but all are now simply designated state parks.

Dead Horse Point State Park near Moab is a sheer-walled elevated peninsula that overlooks much of Canyonlands National Park and a great expanse of Canyon Country to the east of the park, including the La Sal Mountains. The park has paved access, a museum, and a campground.

Green River State Park, adjacent to the town of Green River, is a developed campground and launch area for the small boats and rafts used for running the Green and Colorado rivers.

Newspaper Rock State Park, alongside the state highway that approaches The Needles district of Canyonlands National Park, was established to protect a large panel of Indian petroglyphs. It also offers travelers a small campground.

Goblin Valley State Park, near the state highway that connects Interstate Highway 70 and Hanksville, protects a large area of strangely shaped erosional features. Access is by paved and graded road, and facilities include a developed campground and overlook pavilion.

Anasazi State Park, on a paved road near tiny Boulder, offers a small museum and the remnants of a prehistoric Anasazi Indian village.

Escalante Petrified Forest State Park, accessible by graded road from a state highway just west of Escalante, has a developed campground next to a reservoir and offers hiking trails through a large petrified forest.

Kodachrome Basin State Park, accessible by graded road from Cannonville, is set in a basin of colorful sediments and erosional forms and offers a developed campground.

Coral Pink Sand Dunes State Park, adjacent to a paved road west of Kanab, features a broad expanse of colorful sand dunes and has a developed campground.

Edge of Cedars State Park in Blanding has a museum dedicated to the prehistoric Anasazi Indian culture, and several excavated and restored Anasazi structures.

Goosenecks State Park, an undeveloped promontory that overlooks a serpentine stretch of the San Juan River, is accessible by paved road to the northwest of Mexican Hat.

Monument Valley State Park is an undeveloped section of state land in Monument Valley on the Utah-Arizona line. The paved highway between Mexican Hat, Utah, and Kayenta, Arizona, goes through the reserve.

Goblin Valley State Park
Larry Ulrich

The Colorado River and
Canyonlands National Park
from Dead Horse Point State
Park
Pat O'Hara

BLM SPECIAL AREAS

Left: Grand Gulch Primitive Area
Paul Logsdon

Right: Blue Hills badlands in Utah's Mt. Ellen-Blue Hills Wilderness Study Area
Rodney Greeno

Two large areas in Canyon Country have been set aside by the Bureau of Land Management to protect their outstanding natural and prehistoric values. Both may eventually be given wilderness status.

Dark Canyon Primitive Area is an immense and spectacular canyon system on the western flanks of the Abajo Mountains-Monument Uplift highlands. It is accessible only by backpacking, either from the Colorado River gorge or from primitive roads.

Grand Gulch Primitive Area is a long canyon system that is tributary to the San Juan River. It contains many archaeological sites and is accessible only by backpacking, either from the San Juan River or from the paved road between Mexican Hat and Natural Bridges National Monument.

There are two National Natural Landmarks (NNLs) in Canyon Country. Two detached peaks of the Henry Mountains, Mt. Holmes and Mt. Ellsworth, have been designated the Little Rockies NNL, and the Cleveland Lloyd Dinosaur Quarry in the San Rafael Swell has been given the same status.

The Little Rockies are visible to the southeast from the paved road to Bullfrog Basin on Lake Powell, and can be explored further on foot. The Dinosaur Quarry is accessible by graded road to the south of Price, Utah and is open to the public.

The Bureau of Land Management has designated several areas in Canyon Country as Outstanding Natural Areas (ONAs). Devil's Garden ONA, accessible by graded road south of Escalante, protects a small area of arches and other erosional features.

Escalante Canyons, Phipps-Death Hollow, and The Gulch ONAs are larger areas set aside to protect their outstanding geologic and scenic features. Other than glimpses from roads, access to these areas is limited to hikers and backpackers. All four ONAs are in the upper drainage basin of the Escalante River.

WILDERNESS AREAS

Although many areas in Canyon Country are being considered for wilderness status, only four have been so designated by Congress.

The Paria Canyon-Vermilion Cliffs Wilderness Area is the southern half of the canyon system cut by the Paria River, a tributary of the Colorado River that joins it a few miles below Glen Canyon Dam. The Ashdown Gorge Wilderness Area is adjacent to Cedar Breaks National Monument. The Box-Death Hollow Wilderness Area is near Escalante and lies on the southern flanks of the Aquarius Plateau. The Dark Canyon Wilderness Area lies on the western flanks of the Abajo Mountains-Monument Uplift and includes only the National Forest portion of Dark Canyon. All four areas are outstanding examples of the spectacular, unspoiled canyons so common to Canyon Country. They are accessible only by hiking or backpacking.

Critical decisions about wilderness designation on BLM lands in Canyon Country will be made in the next few years. The agency is currently considering more than 3 million acres of "wilderness study areas" in the state of Utah; the vast majority of it is situated in Canyon Country. According to the BLM, these areas meet the legal criteria for wilderness consideration because they are roadless, "lack substantial human intrusions" and offer "outstanding opportunities for solitude or for primitive recreation."

Some Utah conservationists believe that the BLM has omitted many other areas from wilderness consideration which meet the wilderness study criteria. One coalition of citizen groups has recommended that more than 5 million acres of BLM land in Utah be considered for wilderness.

*Left: The Paria Canyon-
Vermilion Cliffs Wilderness
Area*
F. A. Barnes

*Right: Dark Canyon. The
National Forest portion of Dark
Canyon is a designated
wilderness area*
F. A. Barnes

PARKS THAT GOT AWAY

There are six national parks, seven national monuments, and a number of other special areas in Canyon Country, but had the visions of a few far-sighted men been translated into law, still more of the region's particularly worthy areas would now be protected.

In 1926, in response to urging from a railroad official that a special area in southeastern Utah be set aside as a national monument to promote tourist use of the railroad, National Park Service Director Stephen Mather asked a friend, Dr. Frank R. Oastler, to look over the proposed area and report back. In a letter dated March 13, 1926, Oastler reported favorably on the railroad's proposal and emphasized the importance of granting similar protection to Arch Canyon, east of Natural Bridges National Monument:

Arch Canyon is passed on the way to the White Canyon Bridges. It is really a very remarkable canyon and I am fearful that somebody may obtain a lease of this area and use it for commercial purposes.

In a subsequent letter, Oastler again urged that Arch Canyon be protected by adding it to nearby Natural Bridges National Monument:

This canyon is about 9 miles long and is one of the most beautiful I have ever visited. It would be a shame to have it get into the hands of exploiters.

Following the establishment of Arches National Monument in 1929, Oastler wrote two more letters to the National Park Service in an attempt to determine the status of his suggestion that Arch Canyon be preserved. The Park Service said that the canyon had not been protected because it was partly under Forest Service jurisdiction. Because of this bureaucratic technicality, a magnificent canyon system with unusual natural beauty and numerous prehistoric ruins still lies unprotected and open to degradation.

In a 1975 report summarizing the history of Canyonlands National Park, U. S. Geological Survey geologist S. W. Lohman wrote:

In the 1930's, virtually all of the vast canyon country between Moab, Utah, and Grand Canyon, Arizona, was surveyed for a proposed Escalante National Park. Partly because of the immensity of the area and partly because the name seemingly did not catch on, the proposed park did not get off the ground in the 30's or when a second attempt was made in the 50's.

While some of this vast region has since been given special status, much of it still remains unprotected, and the natural character of many areas has been greatly diminished by mineral development, powerline corridors and other commercial activities.

In a report dated June 1975, the Utah State University College of Natural Resources summarized a detailed survey it had made of the San Rafael Swell in central Utah. The report recommended the establishment of a "San Rafael Swell National Conservation Area," including the "formal designation of the area by Congress." The recommendation was not implemented. With the exception of a few acres, the San Rafael Swell still lies open to a broad range of commercial development activities.

The Henry Mountains
Stewart Aitchison

IV. EXPERIENCING CANYON COUNTRY

$_1H$

Eve
the
wit
high
visi
can
C
high
peri
and
Betw
and
the
and
high
and
T
restr
the
gorg
regi
para
dow
it is
gorg
Vehi
town
O
regio
trave
upri

Hang-gliding at Dead Horse Point.
Frank Jensen

ACCESS AND HIGHWAY TOURING RECREATION

HIKING

Whether it be a short stroll along a marked path in a park or a week-long backpacking trip through a wilderness canyon, hiking in Canyon Country is delightful. The hiking season often lasts all year long due to lack of snowfall in the lower elevations.

Most of the federal and state park areas in the region have developed hiking trails, and the larger ones offer unmarked backpacking routes as well. In non-park areas there are countless routes for both day hiking and overnight backpacking.

Most of the region is arid so the more popular routes are canyon bottoms where springs and streams offer water. Spring water in Canyon Country is generally potable, but most stream water has been contaminated by grazing livestock and is not safe to drink without being properly treated.

Most of the canyons in the region are worth hiking, but a few are exceptional, including Dark Canyon, Grand Gulch, White Canyon, Arch Canyon, Fish Creek-Owl Creek Canyon, Davis Canyon, Lavender Canyon and upper Salt Creek Canyon, all draining from the Abajo Mountains-Monument Uplift highlands; Harts Draw and lower Indian Creek Canyon, which enter Canyonlands National Park from the east; Horseshoe Canyon, part of which is an annex to Canyonlands National Park; Cottonwood Creek and Beaver Creek canyons, both tributaries of the Dolores River gorge; the upper Paria River gorge from near Cannonville, Utah to U.S. 89, and the lower Paria within the Paria Canyon Wilderness Area; and the Escalante River gorge and its many tributaries. Shorter stretches of hundreds of other canyons are just as spectacular.

Most canyons offer little difficulty to hikers but a few present special problems. Canyons cut into certain types of sandstone have not only sheer walls, but may also have undercut drops in their slickrock floors. Ways can be found around some of these drops, but ropes and climbing aids are required for descending or ascending others. Hikers who come prepared for such "aid hiking" will be able to explore canyon systems that are inaccessible to others.

Canyon Country also offers conventional mountain hiking in its island mountain ranges, and two other kinds of hiking found nowhere else. The first, canyon rim hiking, offers breathtaking views into deep and beautiful canyons. This can be challenging where there are numerous side canyons and the rim is irregular. The second type of hiking can be even more challenging. Vast areas of Canyon Country are bare expanses of sandstone eroded into mazes of rounded domes, fins and towers separated by complex networks of narrow crevices, deep gullies and sheer-walled canyons.

Hiking in Buckskin Gulch
Tim Lucas

DESERT CLIMBING

Rock climbing is a popular recreational activity on Canyon Country sandstone. This "desert climbing" requires special skills and entails special risks. Most sandstone breaks or crumbles easily and some sandstone masses contain hidden fractures or joints that can open unexpectedly. At best, sandstone is physically weak rock and desert climbers must allow for this characteristic.

Despite such hazards, Canyon Country climbing is growing in popularity, partly because of the region's spectacular spires and cliff walls. Among the spires that attract desert climbers are several in Monument Valley in the Navajo Indian Reservation; Moses and Zeus in northern Canyonlands National Park; The Titan, one of the Fisher Towers upriver from Moab Valley; Castle Tower, in a tributary canyon of the Colorado River near Moab; and several less spectacular sandstone towers. Extremely challenging walls are found throughout the region. Permits are required for climbing in the Navajo Indian Reservation and in federal or state park areas, but most of the region is open to unrestricted climbing. Access can, however, be a problem since many spires are in remote backcountry areas that can be reached only in four-wheel drive vehicles.

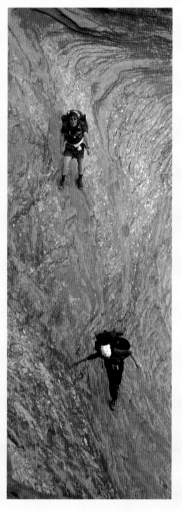

Left: Climbing the "Luxury Liner" along Indian Creek west of Newspaper Rock State Park
Stewart M. Green

Middle: Climbers on Castle Tower in Utah's Castle Valley
Les Ellison

Right: Canyoneering near Navajo Mountain
Rick Reese

ROCKHOUNDING

Rockhounding is popular in Canyon Country, whether it involves a casual finding of "pretty rocks" or a serious search for fossils, mineral specimens and semi-precious gem stones. Canyon Country is a land that has been heavily eroded, making many of its exposed strata convenient "supermarkets" of collectible minerals. All that is required is knowledge of what minerals and fossil specimens occur in each of the geologic layers and the ability to identify and reach locations where these layers are exposed. Abandoned river beds are also sources of fossils and mineral specimens.

Rockhounding in Canyon Country is like walking into a rock shop and finding the specimens neatly arranged on shelves, except that the shelves here are the geologic strata that are so openly exposed. The sediments, chemicals and organic products deposited, the local environmental conditions, and the slow geologic processes that took place over millions of years have combined to create in each ancient rock formation minerals and other specimens quite different from those found in the layers above and below.

The real problem with collecting rocks in Canyon Country is identifying the formations that contain the desired specimens and getting to the places where they are exposed on the surface. Color-coded maps available from the U. S. Geological Survey and other sources identify where these formations are exposed

on the surface. While a few exposures of most formations are within easy walking distance of a highway or road, serious collectors will need some kind of off-road vehicle and detailed maps.

Collecting of any kind is prohibited in national parks and monuments and state park areas. Local maps show where collecting is not allowed, and signs generally indicate their boundaries in the back-country. Limited collecting may be permitted in national recreation areas but officials should be contacted for local regulations. On other public lands, amateur collecting is permitted except for historic and prehistoric artifacts and the intact petrified bones of prehistoric creatures.

Although many Canyon Country geologic strata contain collectible specimens, the most popular formations are:

HONAKER TRAIL FORMATION: abundant marine fossils

CHINLE FORMATION: agate, petrified wood, calcite and barite geodes, jasper, aragonite, selenite, plant fossils, petrified animal tracks and bones, jet, carbonized plantlife and marine fossils in a few locations

SUMMERVILLE FORMATION: agate, chert, jasper, gypsum, animal tracks

MORRISON FORMATION: agate, chert, petrified wood and bone, plant

and invertebrate fossils, calcite, barite, celestite, selenite, geodes, gastroliths, coprolite, and animal tracks

MANCOS SHALE: calcite crystals, aragonite, marine fossils, jet, carbonized plantlife, and some fossil plant impressions in upper layers

IGNEOUS ROCK: copper minerals, silver, gold, smoky quartz and hornblende.

Another source of collectible rock specimens is not so neatly arranged. During the last ten million years, as the Colorado and Green rivers have cut ever more deeply, they have abandoned deposits of water-rounded rock and gravel on benches of rock, some of them hundreds of feet above the present river level. These ancient gravel bars contain very durable rock from every area drained by the rivers and their tributaries.

The Colorado River drains large areas of the Rocky Mountains, the Uncompahgre Uplift, and the La Sal Mountains, while the Green River originates in the Wind River Range of Wyoming and cuts through the Uinta Range and Desolation Canyon before reaching Canyon Country. These high and dry river rock deposits represent an immense and varied geologic area and provide collectors a convenient grab-bag of specimens from which to choose.

Four-wheeling in "The Maze,"
Canyonlands National Park
F.A. Barnes

View from Muley Point, Glen Canyon
National Recreation Area
Jeff Gnass

THE FUTURE OF CANYON COUNTRY

THE FUTURE OF CANYON COUNTRY

Canyon Country's past, both natural and human, has been colorful and unique, but what of its future? The geologic processes that have shaped the land will doubtless continue in their inexorable manner, perhaps modified slightly by mankind's foibles and triumphs. The rocky land will continue to erode, at a rate somewhat accelerated by man's disregard for natural balances, with countless megatons of material carried from its surface each year by flowing water. All of that stupendous mass will now be deposited in Lake Powell behind the Glen Canyon Dam rather than in the Sea of Cortez.

Predictably, deep and lovely Lake Powell will eventually become a 180 mile-long mudflat with the Colorado flowing through a narrow, meandering channel before plunging over the great concrete plug in its inner gorge. The river will then resume filling the next dam downstream, an activity interrupted only briefly by the construction of Glen Canyon Dam.

How soon will Lake Powell become a vast desert swamp? Experts who designed the dam said two centuries, but the Colorado has already proved this estimate wrong. The dam's usefulness may be over by the mid-2000's, a century sooner than planned.

How will those who call Canyon Country home fare in the future? Will their search for economic prosperity and stability be successful? Will this last-explored region of the contiguous United States be developed in ways patterned after the rest of the nation? Will today's descendants of the pioneers who originally settled the region become tomorrow's rural and suburban sophisticates, living high-tech lives in a high-tech world? Or will they cling to their pioneering ways and philosophies in scattered enclaves of traditional America?

To discuss the future it is necessary to analyze some facts and trends of human affairs, both past and present, to consider the people themselves and the values they hold that affect public decisions, and then to extrapolate from these into the uncertain future. The following analysis is based upon the assessments and opinions of scholars and astute observers of the Canyon Country scene.

Slickrock in the Paria Canyon-Vermilion Cliffs Wilderness Area
Gerry Ellis

Glen Canyon Dam
F.A. Barnes

Several factors impose limitations on population and economic growth in Canyon Country. Most are natural, some are political, and one is philosophical.

The natural barriers to economic and population growth are the rugged land itself, its location, and its generally arid climate. The land has imposed severe limitations on the establishment of transportation routes in the area, such as highways and railroads, and the region is geographically remote from major population centers. While much of the readily available water is now used, its natural scarcity will inhibit growth unless it can be used more efficiently.

The principal political limitations on Canyon Country growth are its land ownership pattern and its small, scattered population. With some 90 percent of the land either set aside as Indian reservation or destined to remain under public ownership, there is little room for the land-hungry sprawl of conventional growth. As in the past, the small size of the region's population will continue to limit its impact on political affairs at both the state and federal levels.

The general philosophy that may inhibit Canyon Country growth is the continuing influence of the remnants of a type of frontier thinking on local and state affairs. The pioneering spirit of Americans during the late 1800's and early 1900's enabled them to conquer this remote and rugged land and to establish homes and communities in its few favorable locations. But part of that spirit—the view that the land should be conquered and developed for maximum economic gain—is still present among many of the descendants of those pioneer settlers. In recent decades, this view may have inhibited the realization of the region's unique potential.

This philosophy may now be inappropriate, but it continues to influence public policy in Canyon Country. It has led at times to the pursuit of economic development goals that are neither practical nor cost-effective, or too temporary and cyclical to serve as a stable economic base.

Since Canyon Country was first settled its inhabitants have promoted the development and use of marginal public land for the grazing of domestic livestock. While grazing served an important role in earlier days, it may not be a truly cost-effective business in this region today, and it is unlikely to provide a significant long-term economic base for the area. Sheep grazing on the public lands is perhaps an even more difficult economic proposition.

For most of this century, Canyon Country political leaders have emphasized the development of mineral resources and neglected other promising economic activities. This approach has resulted in a number of boom/bust cycles, each of which has left various communities in a state of economic depression. Mineral development has not provided a sound, long-term economic base for the region. Many of the major minerals found in Canyon Country—coal, oil, uranium and natural gas—can be produced more cheaply elsewhere, and the supply of such non-renewable resources in the region is limited. In a remote and sparsely populated region which lacks available private land, plentiful water, inexpensive power, skilled labor, economic transport, convenient sources of material, and nearby sales outlets, large-scale commercial-industrial development may not be promising.

Padre Bay, Lake Powell, Glen Canyon National Recreation Area.
F.A. Barnes

Despite its limitations, there is an untapped potential in Canyon Country which could signal a promising economic future for the region. The realization of that potential, however, may require changing attitudes and more innovative public policies.

Tourism, travel, recreation, retirement services and facilities and innovative agriculture are probably the best hope for a long-term, stable economic base in Canyon Country. Other more traditional economic activities will, of course, continue at some level, but probably will not provide economic stability. A new mix is needed.

A substantial tourist industry has already evolved in the region, but greater opportunities lie ahead. Tourism is now viewed as largely seasonal, but it should not be. The climate here allows for a long travel and recreation season. Several communities in the region are ideally situated for convention centers which could draw on the great appeal of the unspoiled natural beauty of the area. The climate in many areas of Canyon Country is also highly favorable for retirement living, and development of this economic activity is just beginning.

The movie industry has contributed to the economy in Canyon Country and the makers of print ads and television commercials have recently discovered the country's novel and photogenic landscape. This creative economic activity should be more vigorously pursued. Finally, certain kinds of agriculture have immense growth potential in Canyon Country if the scientific arid-land techniques being developed in other parts of the world, such as drip irrigation and hydroponics, are applied.

The future of Canyon Country can indeed be bright if we will set aside the conventional development concepts of the past and think creatively about new opportunities for the future. Fortuitously, the most promising long-term economic activities for this spectacular region of the west are largely non-consumptive and compatible with the protection of this remarkable landscape.

Aerial view of Natural Bridges National Monument
Fred Hirshmann

Opposite: Dirty Devil Canyon
Michael S. Sample

112

THE AUTHOR

Author-photographer F. A. (Fran) Barnes lives in Moab, Utah in the midst of Utah's Canyon Country and he writes about the region from long personal experience.

After making his own discovery of the region two decades ago, Barnes gave up a career in the aerospace industry and moved to Canyon Country to devote his life to studying, exploring, photographing, and writing about this unique place at the heartland of the Colorado Plateau geologic province.

In the ensuing years Barnes has written and illustrated hundreds of magazine articles about Canyon Country and has designed several commercial maps focusing on two national parks in southeastern Utah. He has authored and illustrated a dozen books about various aspects of the region, and has published an assortment of guide books.

In *Utah Canyon Country* Barnes shares the breadth of his knowledge and his deep interest in this especially spectacular region of the American West.

Autumn pond near Cedar Mesa
Scott S. Warren

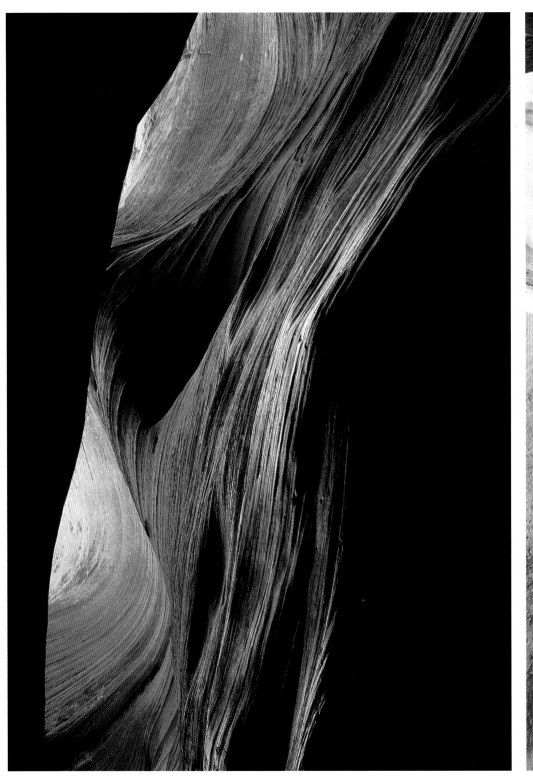

ACKNOWLEDGMENTS

I want most of all to acknowledge the help that my wife of thirty-five years has given in turning my inspired but flawed prose into something readable. Without Terby's tireless patience, this book and the eleven others I have written would probably still be very rough drafts.

I also want to thank my scholarly friend Rodney Greeno for serving as a consultant on certain chapters and for writing the sections on ghost towns, outlaws, the antiquities laws, and the Hole-in-the-Rock expedition. Rodney's shared knowledge and enthusiasm for Canyon Country has helped me produce a better book.

During the research for this book, various individuals in the federal agencies that oversee this vast publicly-owned region have shared with me their specialized knowledge. I am grateful for the assistance of these helpful public servants.

Finally, I would like to thank the Utah Geographic Series for giving me this opportunity to write about and photograph my favorite region. I have long wanted to produce a book that would give readers a conceptual overview of Canyon Country, with a few choice details and a large sample of the chromatic beauty the region has to offer, not as a substitute for seeing it firsthand, but as an introduction that might ultimately lead to an appreciation of this unique land as great and enduring as mine.

Fran Barnes

Opposite left: Rock slot, Echo Canyon, Zion National Park
John Telford

Opposite right: Cane Creek Canyon near Moab, Utah
Tom Till

Aftermath of a storm, Arches National Park
Tom Till

Following page:
This remarkable photo is a portion of a 360° image taken with a slit-scanning panoramic camera from Muley Point on Cedar Mesa. The photo has been cropped to encompass only 234°. The left side of photo is a view to the north and the right side of photo is a view to the southwest. The San Juan River gorge can be seen at center right and Monument Valley on the horizon beyond.
Rod Millar

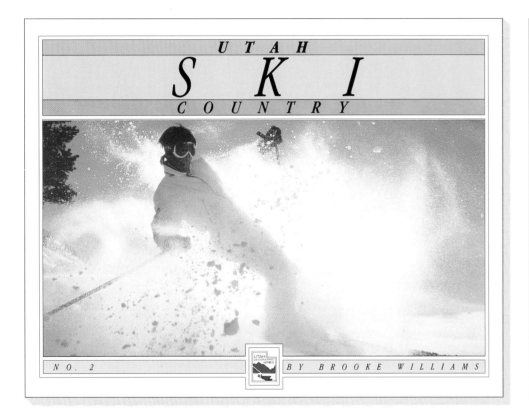

Author Brooke Williams teams up with photographer Chris Noble to bring you the finest book yet on Utah skiing. This stunning volume features 162 color photographs and 25,000 words of authoritative text about *Utah Ski Country.*

Stewart Aitchison, author of *A Naturalist's Guide to Hiking the Grand Canyon* and *A Naturalist's San Juan River Guide*, turns his attention to the wilderness areas of Utah and to the millions of acres currently being considered for wilderness. Nearly 100 color photographs and beautiful maps make *Utah Wildlands* a valuable reference for everyone who shares an interest in Utah's vast wildland treasure.